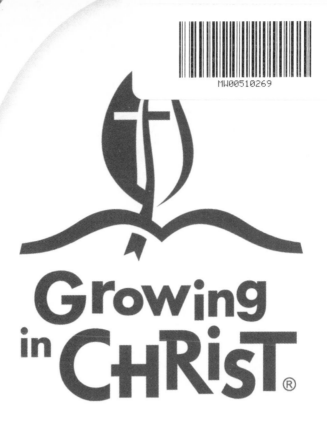

Growing in CHRiST®

Early Childhood
Teacher Guide

CONCORDIA PUBLISHING HOUSE · SAINT LOUIS

Jesus Dies and Rises to Save Us

NEW TESTAMENT 4

Concordia Publishing House
3558 S. Jefferson Ave., St. Louis, MO 63118-3968
1-800-325-3040 • www.cph.org

Written by Marlene Krohse (Lessons 1, 3, 5, 11, and 12), Gail Pawlitz (Lesson 2), Jessemyn Pekari (Lessons 4 and 10), Christine Behnke (Lessons 6–9), and Jeanette Dall (Lesson 13) in consultation with Lorraine Groth

Edited by Lorraine Groth

Cover art © CPH/Greg Copeland

Manufactured in the United States of America

Growing in Christ® is published by Concordia Publishing House. Your comments and suggestions concerning this material are appreciated. Email us at sundayschool@cph.org.

Contents

Lesson	Title	Page	Date of Use
	Introduction	5	
1	Jesus and Zacchaeus	7	_____
2	The Triumphal Entry	15	_____
3	The Widow's Offering	25	_____
4	The Lord's Supper	35	_____
5	Peter Denies Jesus	45	_____
6	The Passion of Christ	55	_____
7	The Resurrection of Jesus	63	_____
8	The Empty Tomb	71	_____
9	Jesus Appears on the Emmaus Road	81	_____
10	Jesus Appears to Thomas	91	_____
11	Jesus Appears in Galilee	99	_____
12	Jesus Ascends into Heaven	107	_____
13	John's Vision of Heaven	117	_____
	Songs & Wiggles-Out Rhymes	127	
	Supply List	128	

Introduction

For the New User

Early Childhood is a nonreader level for children in preschool and kindergarten. It includes a Teacher Guide, Teacher Tools (for teachers), and Student Pack (for children).

Features of the Teacher Guide

- Easy-to-use, four-step weekly lesson plans
- A weekly Bible study on the first page of each lesson to help the teacher prepare
- Reproducible student Activity Pages in each lesson
- Age-appropriate ways to teach the Bible story and apply it to young lives
- Themed snack suggestions in each lesson
- Songs, wiggles-out rhymes, and great ideas to involve children in active learning
- Quarterly supply list at the back of the book
- Perforated pages to make team teaching or small-group/large-group teaching easier

Teacher Tools

This packet provides the following resources for effective teaching:

- **Posters** (teaching aids and Bible story posters)
- **Storytelling Figures** (four pages of story figures for telling the Bible stories)
- **Bible Story Background Tent** (two background scenes to use with the story figures)
- **Attendance chart**
- **CD** (recordings of hymns, songs, Bible Words, and Bible stories; melody-line scores for all music on the CD, Activity Pages, Resource Pages, and a list of student Bible Words in PDF format; and song lyrics in RTF format)

Student Pack

You will need one for each child. This packet includes the following materials:

- **Student Book** (Lesson Leaflets and Craft Pages and a list of the Bible Words at the back of the book to send home with the children)
- **Sticker Pages** (three pages with perforated sections for each lesson)
- **CD** (songs, hymns, catechism songs, and Bible memory words songs)

Additional Teaching Helps

Call 1-800-325-3040 for subscription and cost information to order these helps:

- *Little Ones Sing Praise* (*LOSP*) songbook
- *Sing & Wonder* (*S&W*) songbook
- *Wiggle & Wonder: Bible Story Rhymes and Finger Plays* (*W&W*)
- *Happy Times,* a magazine for young children
- **Puppets**—find an assortment of fun puppets online at cph.org; Jelly can be used interchangeably with Sprout
- **Restickable glue stick**—to allow for repeat use in attaching storytelling figures to backgrounds (order online or at cph.org, or find in the office supply section of your local discount store)
- **Church Year Worship Kit**—a great resource for teaching children about the Church Year (includes a Leader Guide, an altar poster with paraments, prayer posters, and a CD)

Early Childhood Format

Young children need a safe environment with predictable routines and the same caring adults each week to feel secure. For this reason, we recommend letting them learn in their own space, separate from the rest of your program, where they can relax, play, and engage in age-appropriate activities.

You can still make choices in how you organize your Sunday School session and space. Choose the option that works best for your program, or tailor the material to work for your local situation.

Option 1

This format works well if you just have one group of children with one teacher (or a teacher and helper). It is a traditional self-contained classroom where the teacher does all the activities with the whole group of children. If this format suits you, begin with the Welcome Time learning activities and progress through the lesson as it is written, adapting the materials to fit your time frame and children's needs.

Encourage parents to do the Activity Page with their child before they leave. This helps children transition into the classroom. It also helps parents understand what the lesson will be about so they can talk later with their child about what he or she learned. If a grown-up cannot stay to do the activity, enlist a classroom helper to work with the child and adapt the talk accordingly.

Make copies of Activity Page Fun (available in the Teacher Guide and on the Teacher CD) before class so each parent or helper has one. Set these out with copies of the Activity Page and the other supplies they'll need. If your session is under an hour, omit the Welcome activities and start with the opening worship or Bible story.

Option 2

If you have a large number of children in your early childhood program, try a large-group, small-group format. In this approach, children gather in their own class-rooms or designated space to do the Welcome Time learning activities. These learning activities help children transition into the classroom and activate prior knowledge, building interest and readiness for what children will learn in the lesson. Encourage parents to do the Activity Page with their child during this time before going to their own Bible study session.

When it is time to begin, all children in your early childhood program gather with their teachers in one location for the opening worship ("Gathering in God's Name"). Stay in this location to have a teacher tell the Bible story to the whole group, or have children go back to their own classrooms again for the Bible story ("God Speaks"), told by their classroom teacher.

Teachers can do the "We Live" life-application activities in their classroom with their small group of children. Or you can set up each activity as a station. Children divide into small groups and rotate to these stations or sites. Then all preschoolers through kindergartners come back together again for the closing.

Abbreviations

LSB = *Lutheran Service Book* (Concordia Publishing House, 2006)
LOSP = *Little Ones Sing Praise* (Concordia Publishing House, 1989)
W&W = *Wiggle & Wonder* (Concordia Publishing House, 2012)
S&W = *Sing & Wonder* (Concordia Publishing House, 2015)
TG = Teacher Guide

Preparing the Lesson

Jesus and Zacchaeus

Luke 19:1–10

Key Point

Like Zacchaeus, we are among the lost whom the Son of Man came to seek and to save. Jesus asks us to forgive those who sin against us, as He forgives us, unconditionally.

Law/**Gospel**

I sin when I ignore my own sinfulness and focus on the sinfulness of others, rejecting them because of it. **Christ's blood covers not only my sins but also the sins of every sinner, no strings attached.**

Context

Jesus is on the last leg of His journey to Jerusalem as He passes through Jericho. It is a few days before Palm Sunday (Luke 19:28–40). Having already extended mercy to a blind beggar, a resident of Jericho (18:35–43), Jesus now runs into another resident of Jericho in need of mercy—Zacchaeus. Because tax collectors worked for the Roman government and overtaxed people to pad their own wallets, the Jews detested them as thieves and traitors. Since Zacchaeus was rich and a chief among the tax collectors (19:2), he was the object of particular spite, shunned as a "sinner" (v. 7).

Commentary

Thanks to the well-known ditty about this "wee little man," Zacchaeus has often been portrayed as a sort of patron saint of the height challenged. But this is to miss the point. Short though he was, mammoth were his sins. If he is the patron saint of anyone, it is of those who become rich by sucking the lifeblood out of others. Zacchaeus was in the business that no respectable Jew would consider, indeed, that they would abhor as equal to prostituting oneself to the Romans. To make matters worse, such men often became wealthy, doubly damning them in the eyes of their countrymen.

So when Jesus invited Zacchaeus to come down from his sycamore perch and serve Him supper, "all grumbled," saying, "He has gone in to be the guest of a man who is a sinner" (v. 7). This is as much, or more, an indictment of Jesus as of the tax collector. "How dare He even speak to such filth, much less invite Himself over for a meal with that scoundrel!" the people scowled. For Zacchaeus had not only sinned in general, but he had also sinned against them. He had siphoned off their income. Jesus would be dining in a home built with money stolen from them, eating food purchased with cash that was rightfully theirs. If they wanted Jesus to do anything with Zacchaeus, it was to yank a switch from that sycamore tree and publicly whip him for his greed!

Perhaps because he overheard the grumbling and was moved by repentance and faith, this infamous sinner announced, "Behold, Lord, the half of my goods I give to the poor. And if I have defrauded anyone of anything, I restore it fourfold" (v. 8). What a promise! What faith! As a clear fruit of his own repentance, Zacchaeus astounded everyone by such lavish generosity.

Salvation came to this man not because of his bigheartedness but because of his faith in Jesus, which was evidenced in this giving away of wealth. He is among the "lost" whom the Son of Man seeks, as are we, who are forgiven and called to forgive those who sin against us, no matter how Zacchaeus-like their sins may be.

To hear an in-depth discussion of this Bible account, visit cph.org/podcast and listen to our Seeds of Faith podcast each week.

Lesson 1
Jesus and Zaccheus

Luke 19:1–10

Connections

Bible Words
With You there is forgiveness. Psalm 130:4

Faith Word
Forgiven

Hymn
Glory Be to Jesus (*LSB* 433; CD 2)

Catechism
Office of the Keys and Confession

Liturgy
Confession and Absolution

Take-Home Point
Jesus loves and forgives me.

1 Opening (15 minutes)

Welcome Time

What you do: Before class, set up two activity areas. In one, put out copies of Activity Page 1 and crayons. Make copies of Activity Page Fun (below and on CD) for parents or classroom helpers. Adjust talk as necessary.

In the other area, set out a long piece of paper, cookie cutters of trees, toy people, and play dough. Optionally, supply blocks and vehicle and people figures.

Play the CD from your Teacher Tools. As the children arrive, greet each one. Give them a sticker to put on the attendance chart.

Say Hi, [Scott]. I'm glad to see you! I wonder . . . have you ever been to a parade? Today you'll hear about a time people lined up along the streets to see someone special.

Direct children to the tables where you have the activities. Encourage parents or caregivers to stay and do the welcome activity with their child.

Activity Page Fun Get a copy of the Activity Page. Point to the people.

Say These people are waiting for a parade to begin. How do you think they feel? Can you draw smiles on their faces to show they are happy? In today's Bible story, many people gathered to see someone who was coming to their town. That special someone was Jesus! There is something else hidden in this picture that reminds us of Jesus. Look carefully to see if you can find what it is. Have your child find the hidden crosses and color the page.

MATERIALS NEEDED

1 Opening	2 God Speaks	3 We Live	4 Closing
Teacher Tools Attendance chart CD	**Teacher Tools** Background A Storytelling Figures 1-1 to 1-6	**Student Pack** Craft Page 1 Stickers	**Teacher Tools** CD
Student Pack Attendance sticker	**Student Pack** Lesson Leaflet 1 Sticker	**Other Supplies** Sprout or another puppet Green tissue paper & paper cups or construction paper Paper Plus supplies (optional) Fruit that grows on trees	**Student Pack** Take-home items
Other Supplies Activity Page 1 (TG) Play dough, tree cookie cutters & toy figures Blocks (optional) Resource Page 1 (TG)	**Other Supplies** Activity Page 1 (TG) Bathrobes & towels (optional) *Zacchaeus* Arch Book (optional)		

Active Learning Draw a long road on a large piece of paper, and have the children make trees out of play dough to place along the road. Encourage them to move the people figures up and down the road. *Option:* Make a road out of blocks. Use the vehicle and people figures to reenact a parade. Toy vehicles or blocks can be parade floats.

Use your classroom signal to let the children know it's time to clean up and gather for circle time. Sing a cleanup song (Resource Page 1). Have the children pretend they are going to a parade as they gather.

Gathering in God's Name

What you do: Begin with this opening. To teach about the Church Year, use the materials in the Church Year Worship Kit (see the introduction).

Sing "I'm in God's Family" (*S&W*, p. 58; CD 10) or "Glory Be to Jesus" (*LSB* 433; CD 2)

Say I like to be in Sunday School with all of you friends!

Invite the children to say the Invocation and Amen with you. Tell them "Amen" is the special word we say to ask Jesus to hear our prayers just like He promised.

Begin In the name of the Father and of the Son and of the Holy Spirit. Amen.

Offering Have a child bring the offering basket forward. Sing an offering song. Pray, breaking at each asterisk for children to echo the phrase. Tell children you will say a phrase and then they can pray it back to God.

Pray Dear Jesus,* we know* that You died on the cross for us.* Thank You, Jesus,* for forgiving us.* Help us to forgive other people.* Amen.*

Celebrate Birthdays, Baptism birthdays, and special occasions

② **God Speaks** (20 minutes)

Story Clue

What you do: Use a copy of Activity Page 1 to introduce the story, or find pictures of parades online to show on your tablet device.

Say Some of you made a road and trees out of play dough. Some of you colored a picture like this.

Ask What are these people doing? Yes, they are waiting for a parade. Have you ever done that? What would happen if someone tall came and stood in front of this child? Point to child on page. He wouldn't be able to see, would he? When you're out somewhere and you can't see, what does Mom or Dad or Grandma or Grandpa do to help you? Point to dad holding child. Have you ever sat on someone's shoulder so you could see better at a parade or at the zoo?

Say In our Bible story today, a man wants to see Jesus coming down the road, but he can't see over the other people. There are too many people, and he isn't very tall. So, this man finds a special way to see Jesus. But more important, Jesus sees him!

Bible Story Time

What you do: Use Storytelling Figures 1-1 to 1-6 and Background A. Put the figures in your Bible, and remind the children that this is a true story from the Bible. Use a restickable glue stick (see introduction), double-sided tape, or loops of tape to attach the figures. *Option:* Tell the story using the Arch Book *Zacchaeus* (CPH, 59-1599).

Say Today's Bible story is about a man named Zacchaeus (zack KEY us). Show Zacchaeus (1-2). **Zacchaeus was a little man who lived in a big city. He had a lot of money, but he did not have many friends. He was a tax collector. Many people did not like tax collectors because they took money from the people to give to the government. Often they took too much tax money and kept the extra money for themselves.**

One day, Jesus was coming to Jericho (JEHR ih coe), the city where Zacchaeus lived. Zacchaeus wanted to see Jesus. So he hurried to the street where Jesus would walk. Many other people in Jericho hurried out of their houses to see Jesus too! Soon there was a big crowd of people on the street. Add crowd (1-1). **Everywhere Zacchaeus walked, he bumped into people. Even when he stood on his tiptoes, Zacchaeus couldn't see over their heads because he was too short.**

Zacchaeus wondered what to do. Then he had an idea! Zacchaeus saw a big sycamore tree not far away. Add tree (1-3). **Quickly, Zacchaeus climbed up into the tree and sat on a branch that was hanging over the road.** Replace 1-2 with 1-4. **There he watched and waited to see Jesus.**

Soon Jesus came walking down the road. Add 1-5. **When Jesus got to the tree, He stopped and looked up at Zacchaeus. He said, "Zacchaeus, come down out of the tree right away. I'm going to your house today."**

Zacchaeus was so surprised. He didn't think Jesus would know him! He didn't think Jesus would even like him! Right away, he climbed down out of the tree as fast as he could. Then he took Jesus to his house. Replace all the figures with 1-6. Place crowd (1-1) beside 1-6.

Some of the people who saw this grumbled. "Look!" they said. "Jesus went to the home of a bad man. Doesn't He know that Zacchaeus is a big sinner?" But Jesus knew what He was doing. He was Zacchaeus's Friend and Savior. He wanted everyone to know that He came to forgive those who sin and bring them back to God.

Zacchaeus was sorry for the things he had done wrong. He told Jesus he would give half his money to the poor and that if he had taken too much from anyone, he would give it back plus more. Zacchaeus knew that Jesus loved him, and now he wanted to make Jesus happy too.

We also think and say and do wrong things. But Jesus is our Friend and Savior too. Zacchaeus did not tell Jesus his name, but Jesus came to Zacchaeus and called him by name. Jesus comes to us and calls us by name too.

Ask I wonder . . . when does Jesus do this? Let children give suggestions.

Say **Jesus calls us by name when we are baptized. He talks to us through His Word. He makes us His children and helps us show love. Let's say thank You to our Friend and Savior, Jesus, now.** Do so.

Key Point

Like Zacchaeus, we are among the lost whom the Son of Man came to seek and to save. Jesus asks us to forgive those who sin against us, as He forgives us, unconditionally.

Growing in Christ

Bible Story Review

What you do: Show Lesson Leaflet 1. Ask these questions to review. You will also need crayons and a Jesus sticker to do the activities on the leaflet.

Ask **What is Zacchaeus doing in the tree?** He is waiting to see Jesus.

What does Jesus tell Zacchaeus? "Come down. I'm going to your house."

What does Zacchaeus tell Jesus? "I will give half my money to poor people. If I took too much money from anyone, I will give even more money back."

Who forgives Zacchaeus's sins? Jesus

Review the story using the sidebar activity on side 1. Give children a Jesus sticker. Turn to side 2. Have children draw crosses beside all the people because everyone needs Jesus' forgiveness. *Option:* Act out the story with the children. Use some old towels or bathrobes for costumes. Optionally, have the children place the storytelling figures on the board as you retell the story.

Say **Let's act out our story. One day, a big crowd of people gathered along the road.** Crowd gathers. **They were waiting to see Jesus.** Shade eyes, looking for Jesus. **Along came a man named Zacchaeus.** Zacchaeus walks up. **Zacchaeus couldn't see over the other people. He was too little.** Zacchaeus stands on tiptoes or jumps up and down to see. **So, he climbed a tree.** Pretend to climb. **Soon Jesus came down the road.** Jesus walks near, looks up at pretend tree.

Jesus said, "Zacchaeus, come down! I'm going to your house today." Then Jesus and Zacchaeus walked to Zacchaeus's house. Walk.

Sing "Zacchaeus" (*LOSP*, p. 55)

Say **Some of the people grumbled.** Have children grumble. **But Zacchaeus told Jesus, "I'm sorry for all the wrong things I've done."** Shake head repentantly. **Jesus forgave Zacchaeus.** Have Jesus hug Zacchaeus. **Zacchaeus was happy to know that Jesus loved and forgave him. Jesus loves and forgives us too.** Give self hug. **He helps us to show love for others.** Talk about or act out ways to do that, remembering that it is Jesus' love and forgiveness for us that motivate us to respond in love.

Active Learning Idea

Bible Words

What you do: Read Psalm 130:4 from your Bible so children learn that these words are God's Word to us.

Say **Zacchaeus was a sinner. Do you think Zacchaeus was surprised that Jesus stopped to talk to him?** Accept answers. **Jesus showed Zacchaeus that He loved him. He called Zacchaeus by name and told him that He was going to his house. Zacchaeus was sorry for his sins, and Jesus forgave him.**

The Bible says, "With You there is forgiveness" (Psalm 130:4). **God sent His Son, Jesus, to pay for our sins on the cross. Jesus calls us by name and makes us His children through Baptism and His Word. He forgives us when we sin. Let's say our Bible Words together.** Do so.

Say **With You** *Point up.*
there is forgiveness. *Make a cross with your fingers.*

3 We Live (20 minutes)

Help children grow in their understanding of what the Bible story means for their lives. Choose the activities that work best with your class.

Growing through God's Word

What you do: Use Sprout or another puppet.

Sprout: *(Sprout appears to be crying.)* I'm in so much trouble!

Teacher: Why? What happened?

Sprout: Well, Lily and I were visiting our grandma. She lives where it's cold and snowy! We had a lot of fun playing in the snow. We made a big snow-man with a hat and everything. Then Lily went inside, but I stayed outside to write in the snow.

Teacher: That all sounds like fun. So why are you in trouble?

Sprout: Well, I made a big mistake. I used a stone to draw pictures in the snow on my grandma's car. I even wrote our names! Last night, my grandma called. She said there were scratches on her car. And the scratches looked like they said "Sprout and Lily." I'm just a little guy. I didn't know the rock would scratch the car! I was afraid, so I lied and said I didn't do it—Lily did.

Teacher: Oh, Sprout. I know you were scared, but lying is never a good idea.

Sprout: Yeah, I know. Lily will be mad at me when she finds out I said she did it. And my grandma will be mad at me. And my mom will be mad at me. And my dad will be mad at me. That's why I'm in a lot of trouble.

Teacher: This is a problem, Sprout, but you can be forgiven.

Sprout: Really? What should I do?

Teacher: First, you should pray and ask Jesus to forgive you.

Sprout: Maybe Jesus won't want to forgive me. I did a really bad thing. I didn't mean to scratch the car, but I shouldn't have lied about it. Is that a sin?

Teacher: Yes, it is, but Jesus will forgive you. He forgives all our sins. You need to talk to your mom and tell her you are sorry too. She'll help you.

Sprout: No, she'll be mad!

Teacher: She might be angry with you, but I think she will forgive you. You can tell your grandma and Lily that you're sorry and ask them to forgive you too.

Sprout: Okay. I'm sorry that I sinned. But I feel better knowing that Jesus for-gives me! Maybe I can do something nice for my grandma and Lily to show them I'm sorry.

Craft Time

What you do: You will need Craft Page 1, stickers, crayons or green tissue paper, and paper cups or construction paper.

Give the children pieces of tissue paper to glue to the tree for texture, or crayons to color their trees. Give children sticker clothes for Sprout and Lily. Cut out the figures. Fold them on the fold lines to make the figures self-stand-ing, or tape them to upside-down cups to make storytelling figures.

Growing in CHRiST

Preparing the Lesson

The Triumphal Entry

Mark 11:1–10; Luke 19:28–40

Key Point

The multitudes called out "Hosanna!"—Save us!—to their King. We, too, cry out "Hosanna!" to Jesus, our King, who entered Jerusalem to save us and all people by triumphing over sin.

Law/**Gospel**

Sin brought death into the world for me and all people. **Jesus, the perfect Son of God, came to be my Savior and King, dying in my place and rising three days later to save me from sin and give me new life in His kingdom.**

Context

At Jesus' Baptism, God declared Him to be the bearer of the sins of the whole world. For three years, He preached, taught, and worked miracles to show the people that the Old Testament promise of the Messiah had come true. Now, in the last week of His earthly ministry, Jesus "set His face to go to Jerusalem" on His way to the cross (Luke 9:51).

Jesus entered Jerusalem from a small town near the Mount of Olives called Bethphage. It was a town near Bethany, where Mary, Martha, and Lazarus lived.

Commentary

Jesus chose to enter the city on a donkey, displaying the humble nature of His incarnation. He did not come into this world to sit on an earthly throne and rule over an earthly kingdom. He did not ride into King David's city to restore King David's earthly kingdom. If He wanted to do this, He would have ridden on a warhorse, leading an army of soldiers to fight the Romans, who occupied not only Jerusalem but all of the land of Israel. Jesus' kingdom is not of this world.

Instead, Jesus entered upon a donkey and was followed by a multitude that included the poor, the destitute, and even children. They were people who had been waiting to be rescued from their sins. Many in the crowd believed the Old Testament prophecies that the Messiah would be David's son and would come to them humble, riding on a donkey, as the prophet Zechariah had written, "Rejoice greatly, O daughter of Zion! Shout aloud, O daughter of Jerusalem! Behold, your king is coming to you; righteous and having salvation is He, humble and mounted on a donkey, on a colt, the foal of a donkey" (9:9). Animals that had not yet been used were especially appropriate for holy purposes. Jesus was not coming with the riches of an earthly king. No, He rode into Jerusalem with the accolades of a messianic, heavenly king, coming to give the people righteousness and salvation, forgiveness from their sins. This was the first time Jesus allowed people to treat Him as a king.

In a display of divine knowledge, Jesus described to His disciples where and how to find the donkey He would ride. After spreading their cloaks on the donkey, the disciples led the procession into Jerusalem, and the crowds followed. They shouted, "Hosanna! Blessed is He who comes in the name of the Lord!" (Mark 11:9). *Hosanna* means "save us now." The spreading of garments and palm branches is a ceremony of honor, respect, and reverence.

We know something about this crowd from the Gospels. Luke records that the people were rejoicing and praising God for all the great works that they had seen. John 12:17–18 expands on what these works were. These people, or at least a portion of them, had witnessed Jesus raising Lazarus from the tomb after he had been dead four days. The feeding of the five thousand happened just before Jesus "set His face to go to Jerusalem," so those people were also on their way up to Jerusalem at this time.

All of Jesus' ministry led up to this point. In fact, all of Holy Scripture anticipated this moment when God would save His people from their sins in Jesus.

To hear an in-depth discussion of this Bible account, visit cph.org/podcast and listen to our Seeds of Faith podcast each week.

Lesson 2

The Triumphal Entry
Mark 11:1–10; Luke 19:28–40

Connections

Bible Words
Hosanna! Blessed is He who comes in the name of the Lord! Mark 11:9

Faith Word
Hosanna

Hymn
Glory Be to Jesus (*LSB* 433; CD 2)

Catechism
Apostles' Creed: Second Article

Take-Home Point
Jesus is my Savior and King.

1 Opening (15 minutes)

Welcome Time

What you do: Before class, set up two activity areas. In one, set out copies of Activity Page 2A, squares of green paper, glue sticks, craft sticks, a stapler, scissors, and tape. Make copies of Activity Page Fun (below and on CD) for parents or classroom helpers. *Option:* Cut out the palms ahead of time.

In another area, set out plastic Easter eggs and shaker items (e.g., paper clips, dried beans, or aquarium gravel) in disposable bowls with a spoon for scooping. Put out tape, a permanent marker, and a variety of stickers for decorating.

As children arrive, play the CD from your Teacher Tools. Greet children by name. Give them a sticker to put on the attendance chart.

Say Hi, [Colton]. Are you ready to find out more about Jesus, our Savior and King? I wonder . . . what does King Jesus do?

Direct children to the tables where you have the activities. Encourage parents or caregivers to stay and do the welcome activity with their child.

Activity Page Fun Get a copy of the Activity Page 2A and decorating supplies. Show the palm branch outline to your child.

Say Today you'll hear how people waved palm branches and shouted "Hosanna!" to Jesus. *Hosanna* is a special praise word that means "Save us!" Let's make a palm branch to wave and praise Jesus too. Help your child glue green squares to the palm branch. Trim and staple it to a craft stick handle. Cover the back of the staples with tape. Write child's name on the palm.

© 2017 Concordia Publishing House. Reproduced by permission. Available on the Teacher CD.

MATERIALS NEEDED

1 Opening	2 God Speaks	3 We Live	4 Closing
Teacher Tools Attendance chart & CD	**Student Pack** Lesson Leaflet 2	**Student Pack** Craft Page 2 & stickers	**Teacher Tools** CD
Student Pack Attendance sticker	**Other Supplies** Activity Page 2A (TG)	**Other Supplies** Cross & crown	**Student Pack** Take-home items

Other Supplies
Activity Page 2A (TG)
Green paper squares
Craft sticks, spoons & bowls
Plastic Easter eggs, 1 per child;
  items to shake & stickers
Resource Page 1 (TG)
	Mystery bag, cross & paper
	  crown
	Donkey (pool noodle, hobby
	  horse, or the like)
	White T-shirt & blankets
	Palm branches
	Jesus Enters Jerusalem Arch Book
	  (optional)
		Sprout or another puppet
		Wide ribbon
		Toy figures & blocks (optional)
		Activity Pages 2B & 2C & Paper
		  Plus supplies (optional)
		Stick pretzels & paper plates
			Other Supplies
			Celebration shakers & palms

Active Learning Make celebration eggs. Give each child one plastic egg. Show the children how to take turns and scoop small shaker items into half the egg. Help them join the two halves. Secure the edges with tape. Label the eggs with a permanent marker. Children may decorate the eggs with stickers of smiley faces, crosses, hearts, flowers, and the like.

When the eggs are finished, use them to praise God. Tell the children to stand, shake the eggs loudly, and say, "Hosanna! Blessed is He who comes in the name of the Lord." Ask them to repeat the words softly. Finally, have them march around the room, shaking the celebration eggs to accompany words of praise to Jesus, our Savior and King.

Say **Long ago, children and adults welcomed Jesus into Jerusalem by laying down coats, waving palms, and shouting, "Hosanna! Blessed is He who comes in the name of the Lord!"** (Mark 11:9). **Today, we welcome Jesus as our Savior and King with joyful sounds. Jesus is our Savior. Jesus is our King. Jesus is the Ruler of everything!**

Option: Instruct children to line up in parallel lines, cheering as one student walks between the lines. The crowd says, "Save us, King!" Allow time for each child to have a turn as the king. Then tell the children that in today's Bible story, people gathered along a road to cheer for King Jesus.

Use your classroom signal to let the children know it's time to clean up and gather for circle time. Sing a cleanup song (Resource Page 1).

Say **Pretend you are riding a donkey as you come to our story area.**

Gathering in God's Name

What you do: Gather the children, and begin with this opening. To teach about the Church Year, use the materials in the Church Year Worship Kit (see the introduction for more information).

Sing "Hosanna! Hosanna!" (*LOSP*, p. 94) or "Glory Be to Jesus" (*LSB* 433; CD 2)

Say **I like to be in Sunday School with you, my royal friends! Today we'll learn that Jesus is our Savior and King!**

Invite the children to say the Invocation and Amen with you. Tell them "Amen" is the special word we say to ask Jesus to hear our prayers just like He promised.

Begin **In the name of the Father and of the Son and of the Holy Spirit. Amen.**

Offering Have a child bring the offering basket forward. Sing an offering song. Have children echo each phrase after the asterisk in the prayer.

Pray **Dear Jesus,* help me listen* to Your Word.* Help me rejoice* because You are* my Savior and King.* Amen.***

Celebrate Birthdays, Baptism birthdays, and special occasions

 **2 God Speaks** (20 minutes)

Story Clue

What you do: In a mystery bag, hide a cross and paper crown.

Say Now it is time for some story clues. Today I have two things in this mystery bag. They are clues to help you think about a person in today's Bible story. Let's check out the clues. Pull out the crown. **Oh, look. What do you think of when you see this crown?** Accept answers. **You might be right. We'll find out later. Now let's see what else I have in this mystery bag.** Invite a child to pull out the cross. **Look. It's a cross. Whom do you think of when you see a cross? I wonder if the cross and crown are clues to the same person. Let's be great Bible detectives and find out!**

Bible Story Time

What you do: Use a large white T-shirt, several blankets, the palm branches made during Welcome Time, and a pretend donkey (a pool noodle or the like).

ive Learning Idea!

Choose one student to be Jesus and ride the "donkey." Other children sit quietly along both sides of a blanketed path, prepared to stand, wave their palms, and cheer. *Option:* Show the pictures in the Arch Book *Jesus Enters Jerusalem* as you tell the story (CPH, 59-1585).

Say **One day close to the Passover celebration, Jesus was making plans to ride into the city of Jerusalem. He asked two of His disciple-friends to go and get a special young donkey no one had ever ridden. The two disciples went and did just what Jesus asked them to do.** Show the donkey you will use. **When the two men returned with the donkey, some disciples threw their coats on the donkey's back. Then Jesus climbed on and started riding to Jerusalem.** Ask the child playing Jesus to get "on" the donkey and walk slowly along the pathway.

Clip-clop, clip-clop **went the donkey's hooves. Jesus rode closer and closer. Crowds were waiting for Him.** *Clip-clop, clip-clop.* **The people saw Jesus coming and started cheering.** Ask the children playing the bystanders to get up and wave their palms.

Some people put down their coats to honor Jesus. Others cut palm branches and waved them back and forth. *Swish-swish, swish-swish* **went the palm branches.**

The happy people shouted, "Hosanna! Blessed is He who comes in the name of the Lord!" Repeat the words with the children as they wave their branches. **The people cheered for Jesus to save them and be their king on earth. Jesus was their king, but not the way the people thought. Jesus had a better plan to save them.** Tell the children to sit down.

Later that week, Jesus would die on the cross as our Savior King. Jesus would die for the sins of all people. And three days after His death, Jesus would come alive and show His power over death. He died and rose again for us too. He deserves our praise. He is our Savior and King too. Invite children to wave palms or their arms.

Bible Story Review

What you do: Have leaflets and crayons ready to hand out. Hold up Lesson Leaflet 2 as you review using the questions and picture on the leaflet.

Ask **What are the people waving?** Palm branches

What are the people saying? "Hosanna! Blessed is He who comes in the name of the Lord!" [Mark 11:9].

Key Point

The multitudes called out "Hosanna!"—Save us!—to their King. We, too, cry out "Hosanna!" to Jesus, our King, who entered Jerusalem to save us and all people by triumphing over sin.

Growing in CHRIST.

Where is Jesus going? He is riding into Jerusalem on a donkey.

How can you praise Jesus? Accept answers.

Hand out leaflets and crayons. Read the words in the sidebar, and have the children find the items listed. Encourage the children to talk about ways they, too, can praise Jesus. On side 2, help the children find the dot-to-dot pictures of a cross and crown and color them. Remind the children that Jesus is also their King and their Savior.

Option: Join together for the "Do Together" praise action on the leaflet. Use the celebration eggs made earlier in the lesson.

Bible Words

What you do: Read the Bible Words from Mark 11:9: "Hosanna! Blessed is He who comes in the name of the Lord!"

Say **Our Bible Words today are from our Bible story. They are happy words. Let's stand and say them. Raise your hands in the air and say, "Hosanna!" This word means "Save us!" Jesus did just that. He came to save those people and us, too, from sin, death, and the power of the devil. Let's raise our hands in the air and say "Hosanna" again.** Do so. **Now we can march in place and say our Bible Words. Watch me first.**

Say the Bible Words as you march in place.

Say **Blessed is He who comes in the name of the Lord!** Then tell the children to march and say the words twice.

Now let's put together the first part and the last part to say our Bible Words. Watch me. Then do what I do too. Repeat the Bible Words again, raising hands and marching in place.

Option: Use the celebration eggs or palms made earlier in this lesson. Video-record the children saying the Bible Words and using their eggs. Email the video to parents this week to let them know what their child is learning in Sunday School.

3 We Live (20 minutes)

Help children grow in their understanding of what the Bible story means for their lives. Choose the activities that work best with your class.

Growing through God's Word

What you do: Use the Bible story clues (cross and crown) and Sprout.

Sprout: Hi, Teacher. Hi, kids. What are you doing?

Teacher: Hi, Sprout. I'm glad you came. We are talking more about our Bible story and our clues.

Sprout: Clues? Oh, boy! A mystery. Should I get my magnifying glass?

Teacher: Oh no. You won't need that. I already have the clues. The first one is a crown. (*Show the crown.*)

Sprout: I know what the crown means. It is something a king wears. But was Jesus really a king, a ruler?

Teacher: He was. But Jesus was not like the other kings the people knew. Those kings had armies and fancy crowns. Jesus had no armies. He came to earth from heaven to win a battle over sin and death by living without sin. At just the right time, Jesus gave up His life on the cross in our place. *(Show the cross.)*

Sprout: Is that why you have that cross too?

Teacher: It sure is. Jesus died for the sins of all people. He is our Savior and King. So that is super good news for the children and for me too. Thanks for letting us share it, Sprout. You are a good detective, but then so am I, because right now, I hear your mom calling you. I think she needs your help too.

Sprout: Okay. I better scoot. Bye, boys and girls. *(Sprout waves good-bye. Children can reciprocate.)*

Say **Most of you know Sprout is a puppet friend. He isn't real. But we are real. We are really God's children. We are members of God's kingdom. We can really pray, praise, and give thanks to our Savior King in many ways. Let's do some of that now. I'll say something boys and girls might do. If you think it is a good way to praise God, wave your fingers like this.** Demonstrate. **If you don't think it is good, make a cross with your fingers to remember Jesus forgives the things we think and say and do that are wrong. Jesus is our Savior.** Demonstrate. Begin listing items.

Sing songs of praise. *Wave.*

Talk to your friends during the Bible story instead of listening. *Make cross.*

Poke your neighbor instead of praying. *Make cross.*

Be happy while helping others. *Wave.*

Thank God for family and friends. *Wave.*

Say **You were good listeners. And you had the right answers. We need a Savior, and we need a King. Jesus is both. He is our Savior and King. He can take care of everything. The children long ago shouted, "Hosanna! Blessed is He who comes in the name of the Lord!" We can do that too.**

Optional: If you have time, ask the children to tell different ways that Jesus takes care of them. Give examples, such as "Jesus gives me food."

Craft Time

What you do: Use Craft Page 2, the stickers of Jesus for this lesson, and crayons to make a table tent figure of Jesus riding the donkey. Set out lengths of wide ribbon to serve as roads. *Optional:* Have the children line the ribbon with people figures and build Jerusalem with blocks.

Say **In today's Bible story, Jesus rode on a donkey into a special town called Jerusalem. He went there to celebrate Passover. Along the road, people gathered to cheer for Jesus.**

Ask **What did the people shout?** Let children tell.

Say **Yes, "Hosanna! Save us!" Jesus is our Savior and King too. He is the Ruler of heaven and earth. He died on the cross for our sins. We can celebrate too!**

Growing in CHRiST

The Triumphal Entry

Jesus is riding into Jerusalem.

❶

Hosanna!

❷

Cut

Directions

Use Activity Pages 2B and 2C to make an accordion-foldout storybook.

First, cut Activity Page 2B on the two solid lines to separate booklet pictures from the directions. Prefold the picture strip on the dashed line so the pictures are on the inside. Cut Activity Page 2C in half on the center solid line. Trim edges at both solid lines. Prefold on dashed lines.

Tape picture 2 to picture 3. Tape picture 4 to picture 5. You will have a long strip of pictures that depict the story.

Now, accordion-fold the strip of pictures. Beginning with pictures 1 and 2, fold the Jesus picture down along the dashed line, so the blank side on the back shows on top. This will become the cover of your storybook. Write "Jesus Is My Savior and King" on it. Younger children can draw a crown and/or a cross.

Continue to accordion-fold the pictures. With the title page showing on top, fold that section of pictures under picture 3. Fold all the pictures forward over picture 4. Fold all the pictures back under picture 5. Fold all the pictures forward over picture 6. If done correctly, only your cover will now be showing.

Open to pictures 2 and 3. Use the pictures to tell the story: "Jesus is riding into Jerusalem." Continue to pull the book open so it gets longer and longer with the telling of the story: "Hosanna! Blessed is He who comes in the name of the Lord!" At the end, all of the pictures will show.

Option: Use the story scenes to make puppets. Color and cut out each scene. Glue them to separate upside-down cups. Use the puppets to retell the story.

2

Blessed is He

who comes

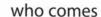

❸

❹

in the name of the Lord!

Hosanna! Hosanna!
Our Savior and King.
Hosanna! Hosanna!
Our praises we bring.

Dear Jesus, thank You for being my Savior and King! I praise You too! Amen.

❺

❻

Preparing the Lesson

The Widow's Offering

Mark 12:41–44

Key Point

The widow gave all she had to God, trusting Him to provide and care for her. Her actions point us to Jesus, who gave His all for us, even though we fail to trust in God for all things.

Law/**Gospel**

I do not always obey God's demand that I love Him with all my heart. I am not willing to give Him all that I have. **Christ loves me and willingly redeemed me, not with gold or silver, but with His holy, precious blood and with His innocent suffering and death that I might be His own and live under Him in His kingdom and serve Him.**

Context

Preceding this story are several incidents that involve Jesus' face-offs with the religious leaders of the day—the Pharisees, Sadducees, and scribes. The Pharisees challenge Him about taxes (Mark 12:13–17); the Sadducees, about the resurrection (vv. 18–27); and the scribes, about the priority of the Commandments (vv. 28–34).

Right before spotting the widow, Jesus dresses down the scribes for strutting about like peacocks in their "long robes" (v. 38), their narcissistic addiction to public praise, and the heartless way they "devour widows' houses" (v. 40). Presumably, Jesus means the way these teachers swindle widows out of their savings, all supposedly in the service of God.

Commentary

The kingdom of heaven is not exemplified by the scribes. They dress, pray, and act piously, but it is all only a ruse. Their outward masks of long robes, long prayers, and seats of honor only disguise their impious interior. Yet they suppose Jesus is impressed with their sanctity, so holy are they. He's not impressed, of course, for Jesus sees things as they really are. In seeking for and savoring human commendation, such people have earned "the greater condemnation" from Him whose eyes pierce through the outward uprightness to the inward depravity (v. 40).

Neither is the kingdom of heaven exemplified by the rich people who dropped large sums into the temple coffer, for "they all contributed out of their abundance" (v. 44). Jesus implies that their contributions are meant primarily to finance their own standing within the community.

Rather, the widow shows what it means to be part of the kingdom of heaven, that is, to live by faith as God's child. When she contributed her "two small copper coins, . . . she out of her poverty . . . put in everything she had, all she had to live on" (vv. 42, 44). She didn't give in fractions, divvying up a little for God, a little for her, and a little for whatever struck her fancy. She gave all. And in that, she is a model for us all. The point is not that we, too, should give all our money to the church. The point is that we should give our all to God—all our love, our devotion, our minds, our everything.

The kingdom of God is not static, but dynamic. It is Jesus' work for us: Jesus in action in the lives of His people. It is often hidden in the smallest of things: in those two tiny coins, given by faith; in the splash of water on the head of a sinner over the font; in the quarter-size piece of bread placed on the communicant's tongue; in the naked King of kings robed only in His own blood on the cross. The drops of His blood, of greater worth than all gold and silver, fall into heaven's treasury. And when His blood in that coffer rings, the angels in heaven sing, "Glory to God in the highest" for He earns peace for His people on earth.

To hear an in-depth discussion of this Bible account, visit cph.org/podcast and listen to our Seeds of Faith podcast each week.

Lesson 3
The Widow's Offering
Mark 12:41–44

Connections

Bible Words
We love because [God] first loved us. 1 John 4:19

Faith Word
Offering

Hymn
Glory Be to Jesus (*LSB* 433; CD 2)

Catechism
Apostles' Creed: First Article

Liturgy
Offering

Take-Home Point
I give an offering to say thank You to God.

 1 Opening (15 minutes)

Welcome Time

What you do: Before class, set up two activity areas. In one, put out copies of Activity Page 3A, coin stickers (Sticker Sheets), and crayons. Make copies of Activity Page Fun (below and on CD) for parents or classroom helpers. Adjust talk as necessary.

In another area, set out large beads, an assortment of coins, or other items to sort or count.

Play the CD from your Teacher Tools. As the children arrive, greet each one. Give them a sticker to put on the attendance chart.

Say Hi, [Ellarose]. How are you? Have you been to church yet? Do you like to give money when there is an offering in church? Today we're going to learn about a woman who gave an offering to God.

Help child get started in one of the following activities to build interest and readiness for the lesson. Encourage parents or caregivers to do an activity with their child.

Activity Page Fun Get a copy of the Activity Page, three coin stickers, and crayons. Have your child trace the rim of the offering plate, add sticker coins to it, and color the page. Talk about the picture.

Ask What is the boy doing? Yes, he is giving an offering in church. In the Bible story today, you will hear about a woman who gave an offering to God. How much do you think she gave? Listen and find out.

MATERIALS NEEDED

1 Opening	2 God Speaks	3 We Live	4 Closing

Teacher Tools
Attendance chart
CD
 	
Student Pack
Attendance sticker
Coin stickers
 	
Other Supplies
Activity Page 3A (TG)
Items to count & sort
Resource Page 1 (TG)
	Student Pack
	Lesson Leaflet 3
	
	Other Supplies
	Small lunch bag with dollars &
	  coins inside (play or real)
	Offering basket or plate & play
	  money or coins
	The Widow's Offering Arch Book
	  (optional)
		Teacher Tools
		Poster A
		
		Student Pack
		Lesson Leaflet 3
		Craft Page 3
		Stickers
		
		Other Supplies
		Pennies, stickers, or other gifts
		Gift bag or small box
		Page protectors (optional)
		Activity Page 3B & Paper Plus sup-
		  plies (optional)
		Vanilla wafers
			Student Pack
			Take-home items

Active Learning Encourage the children to sort the items into like piles.

Ask **Which pile has a lot? Which has a little? How many [red beads/nickels] do you have? Count and see. Today, we will hear about a woman who gave all her money to God. Do you think it was a little or a lot?**

Use your classroom signal to let the children know when it is time to clean up. Sing a cleanup song (Resource Page 1). As the children gather, have them sing "Jesus gives us everything, everything, everything, Jesus gives us everything, because He loves us so" to the tune of "Mary Had a Little Lamb."

Gathering in God's Name

What you do: Begin with this opening. To teach about the Church Year, use the materials in the Church Year Worship Kit (see the introduction).

Sing "I'm in God's Family" (*S&W*, p. 58; CD 10) or "Glory Be to Jesus" (*LSB* 433; CD 2)

Say **I am glad to see all you friends in Sunday School today!**

Invite the children to say the Invocation and Amen with you.

Begin **In the name of the Father and of the Son and of the Holy Spirit. Amen. "Amen" is the special word we say to ask Jesus to hear our prayers as He has promised.**

Offering Pass your offering plate (or basket) from child to child to collect the offerings. If you collected them at the beginning of class, give children some pennies to put in now. Sing part of the offertory or an offering song.

Say **God gives us everything. One way we say thank You is by giving an offering in church or Sunday School.**

Pray **Thank You, God, for everything we have. Thank You for sending Jesus to be our Savior. Help us to listen and learn today. Amen.**

Celebrate Birthdays, Baptism birthdays, and special occasions

2 God Speaks (20 minutes)

Story Clue

What you do: Place some coins and dollar bills inside a small lunch bag.

Say **My friend gave me something yesterday. It is inside this bag.** Show bag. **Would you like to see what it is?** Shake bag and let children guess. Then, open bag and show them. **It's money! It was really kind of my friend to give me this money, wasn't it? I didn't work for it, and it wasn't my birthday. She didn't owe me the money; she just gave it to me. It was a gift.**

Ask **What do you think I should do with the money?** Listen to answers.

Say **You know what I think I'll do with this money? I'll use it to buy something for my friend! I am so happy she is my friend! She showed her love for me by giving me this money. I want to show her that I love her too. She gave me a gift, and I'll give her a gift! But first, let's listen to our Bible story today. It is about a woman who gave some money to God.**

Bible Story Time

What you do: You will need an offering plate or basket from church and real or play dollar bills or coins, money from a board game such as Monopoly, or play money you have made by cutting up paper. *Note:* Since young children do not know the value of money, use many coins or bills for the rich people's offering and just a few for the poor people's to indicate the size of the offerings. *Option:* Use *The Widow's Offering* Arch Book (CPH, 59-2214) to tell the story.

Say **The Bible tells us that one day Jesus and His friends, the disciples, were in God's house, the temple. Jesus was sitting near the place where people gave their offering money to God. Jesus watched the people putting their offerings in the big offering containers. Some rich people came and put lots and lots of money into the offering containers. But they had lots more money left. They just gave a little of what they had.**

Today, we put our offerings in a basket or offering plate like this. Show offering plate or basket. **Let's do that now.** Give the children real or play money, and have them put it into your offering plate or basket.

Jesus saw a poor woman walking over to an offering jar. The woman's husband had died. She didn't have very much money. Shake head no. **But the woman trusted God to take care of her. She walked up to the offering container and put in two small coins. Her coins weren't worth even a penny!** Drop one penny into the offering plate. **But they were all she had.**

Ask **Do you think Jesus was happy with this poor woman's gift? Yes, He was! He told His disciples, "This woman is poor, but she gave more than anyone else. The other people gave just a little bit of their money. They still have lots of money left for themselves. But this woman gave all she had."**

Say **Let's think about this story from God's Word. No one made the woman put her money in the offering jar.** Shake head no. **She could have kept it for herself. But she put in all she had.**

Ask **Do you think this is what made Jesus happy?** Shake head no. **No, Jesus was not happy because the woman gave everything she had. Jesus was happy with her gift because she gave it with a thankful heart. The woman knew that God loved her and that everything she had came from Him. She trusted that God would always take care of her. She was thankful for His love, so she wanted to give God a gift to say thank You.**

Say **God loves and cares for us too. He gives us everything we need. He showed how much He loves us when He sent Jesus to be our Savior from sin. We can trust Him to take care of us always. Because He loves us so much, we bring Him our offering gifts to say thank You.**

Bible Story Review

What you do: Show Lesson Leaflet 3, and use the questions to review the story. Then hand out the leaflets and crayons or markers.

Ask **Where are Jesus and His disciples?** In God's house, the temple

What is the woman doing? She is giving an offering.

How does her offering show love for Jesus? She gave all she had. She

---

Key Point

The widow gave all she had to God, trusting Him to provide and care for her. Her actions point us to Jesus, who gave His all for us, even though we fail to trust in God for all things.

Growing in CHRiST.

trusted God to take care of her.

Who gives us everything we need? God

What are some things God gives you? Accept answers.

If you have time, play I Spy with the children.

Say **Let's play I Spy. I'll spy something that comes from God. You listen and see if you can guess what it is.** Give a clue about something children can see (I spy . . .), and have them guess what it is. After exploring ways God cares for us, hand out the leaflets and do the activities on them:

Say **We just talked about some of the good things God gives us. The woman in our Bible story received good things from God too. She was thankful for His love, so she gave an offering to Him. Point to the picture that shows what she gave.** (The two coins) Next, point to dot-to-dot heart. **Now connect the dots.**

Ask **What did you make?** (A heart) **God gives us everything we need because He loves us very much. God gave us what we need most when He sent Jesus to take away our sins. Draw a cross on the heart.** Turn to side 2.

What is the girl doing? (Giving an offering) **God wants us to give out of love too. When we give money to church, we are giving it to God. Color the offering plate and money.**

Bible Words

What you do: Read "We love because [God] first loved us" from 1 John 4:19 in the Bible. Divide children into two groups to say the words or sing "We Love" (*LOSP*, p. 54).

Say **The woman trusted God to take care of her. She was thankful for God's love, so she gave Him an offering of all she had. God loves us and forgives us for Jesus' sake too. He cares for us and gives us everything we have. He helps us show love for others. Let's say our Bible Words together.**

Group 1: We love *(clap, clap)* **because [God] first loved us.**

Group 2: We love *(clap, clap)* **because [God] first loved us.**

Group 1: We love *(clap, clap)***.**

Group 2: We love *(clap, clap)***.**

Together: We love *(clap, clap)* **because [God] first** *(clap)* **loved** *(clap)* **us** *(clap)***.**

3 We Live (20 minutes)

Help children grow in their understanding of what the Bible story means for their lives. Choose the activities that work best with your class.

Growing through God's Word

What you do: You will need an inexpensive gift to give each child (e.g., pennies, stickers, bookmarks, cookies). Put them inside a gift bag or wrapped box. You will also need Poster A. Fold the poster in half to talk about the first two scenes, and unfold it to talk about the last two.

Ask **How many of you like to get gifts on your birthday?** Accept responses. **It is fun to give gifts too. When we care about someone, we like to give them gifts, don't we?** Show bag or box.

Say **I care about you. So, today, I brought something to give each of you.** Give each child one of the items. **It's fun getting a present, isn't it?**

Did you know that everything we have and everything we get really comes from God? Even this present that I gave you really comes from God. He cares for me and gives me what I need. He helped me be able to give these things to you too.

Point to the children on Poster A. **Jasmine and Isaiah are playing outside. Who gives them the sunshine to play in? Yes, God! Can you think of something else that is outside that comes from God?** Accept answers. **God gives us all these things because He loves us.** Point to next picture.

Ask **What are Jasmine and Isaiah doing now? Yes, they are eating lunch. What do you like to eat for lunch?** Listen to answers. **Who gives us our food?** Help children understand that God is the one who sends the rain and gives us sunshine so food will grow.

Say **God gives us food because He loves us so much.** Point to the clothes the children are wearing. Help them understand that clothing is a gift from God too. **God gives us our clothes.** Point to mother. **He gives us moms and dads and family to love us. God gives us everything we need. He does this because He loves us.**

I gave you a little gift because I love you. God loves us much, much more. God knew that we needed a Savior. So, He gave us the gift of His Son. Open poster and point to third picture. **He sent Jesus to die on the cross for us and rise again. Jesus came to pay for our sins so we could have forgiveness and live with Him in heaven someday.** Point to people giving offering.

These people are giving an offering. When we go to church and Sunday School, we can give an offering too. We give an offering because we know that everything we have comes from God. We give an offering to say thank You to God for loving us. We give an offering so that others will learn about Jesus and His love too.

If your Sunday School or church supports specific mission projects, show pictures of these, or tell about them. Consider contacting a missionary to ask if your class could Skype with him or her about what he or she does.

Ask **What are these children doing?** Point to children singing in a choir. **They are singing in the choir. They are giving an offering too. They are using their voices to sing praise to God.**

What else can we give God besides our money? Encourage children to think of ways they can serve their neighbor through their time and talents. **All these things are ways that we show our love for God and others.**

Craft Time

What you do: You will need Craft Page 3, crayons or markers, and stickers to make place mats. *Option:* Put finished place mats into see-through page protectors.

Say We're going to make a place mat today. You can take it home and use it when you eat. It will help you remember all the things that God gives us because He loves us. Look at the side with the prayer. **Can you name something you see on the place mat that God has given us?** Accept answers.

Give children picture stickers to add to their place mats. Read the prayer. Side 2 shows ways God the Holy Spirit works in us to help us show love for God and others. Have the children connect the dots, color the cross, and read the Bible Words. Talk about the pictures and give the children a heart sticker to add to each scene. Talk about how we can also show love by giving an offering of our time, talent, or treasure.

Paper Plus option: Make paper banks. Give each child an enlarged copy of Activity Page 3B, tape, and crayons. Have children color and assemble the cube according to the directions on the page. If desired, supply boutique-style tissue boxes for durability. Cut the scenes apart, and tape or glue one to each side of the box.

Direct them to draw money in the offering plate. Discuss the cross shape, asking the children what it is. Remind them that Jesus loved us so much that He died on the cross for us. Help the children to fold the cross into a bank. They can put their money in it to give an offering to God to say thank You for His love. Read the words on each scene of the cube. Help children understand how their offerings are used by your church to tell others about Jesus.

Snack Time

What you do: Give each child two vanilla wafers. Use the prayer on the Craft Page. Discuss ways they can show love in what they do and say.

Live It Out

What you do: Encourage children to teach their parents or someone else this week's Bible Words. Use the actions too.

4 Closing (5 minutes)

Going Home

What you do: Send home take-home pages and crafts.

Say The woman gave all she had to God because she knew God loved her and that everything comes from Him. We can give an offering to say thank You to God too. Say take-home point together.

Sing "Father, Bless the Gifts We Bring You" (*LOSP*, p. 22) or "We Love" (*LOSP*, p. 54)

Pray Dear Jesus, everything we have is a gift from You. Help us want to give our offerings to You because we know You love us. Amen.

Reflection

Good stewardship often begins when we're young and realize that all we have is a gift from God so that everything we do in faith to the glory of God or for the benefit of our neighbor is an offering. What activities helped promote this idea? What might you do differently in the future to encourage this idea?

Add an offering to the offering plate.

My Offering

Each day, I'll add another.
Then, count them one by one.
They will help a pastor
Tell what God has done.

I'll add a little quarter,
Even though it's small.
It will help to buy a Bible
That tells God's love for all.

Enlarge and copy cross on heavy paper. Color or decorate it.

Cut out the cross on solid lines and fold on dotted lines to assemble. Tape in place. The top flap will fold over the top of the box. Cut solid line under song to make a slit. Leave flap open to take out the money, or tape closed with removable tape for a "bank." Open flap to take money out. Read the panels, and talk about how church offerings are used.

Option: Cut out the square panels and glue them to the six sides of a boutique-style tissue box.

We love because [God] first loved us. 1 John 4:19

Father, bless the gifts
  we bring You;
Give them something
  good to do.
May they help someone
  to love You;
Father, may we love You too.

Cut.

Preparing the Lesson

The Lord's Supper

Luke 22:1–23

Key Point

Jesus is our Passover Lamb, who with His very body and blood grants us forgiveness, life, and salvation.

Law/**Gospel**

I betray my Lord when I sin. **Jesus is the Lamb of God who takes away the sin of the world. With His very body and blood, He grants me forgiveness, life, and salvation.**

Context

It is very helpful for understanding the Last Supper to read and be familiar with the original Passover story in Exodus 12. The Feast of Unleavened Bread commemorated that original Passover event every year in the springtime. This feast was observed in homes, among family and friends. The main elements of this feast were a communal meal of lamb and unleavened bread and a recounting of the deliverance of God's people through the first Passover.

Commentary

By this time in Jesus' ministry, the religious leaders of the Jewish people were united in their opposition to Jesus (v. 2). The question was not whether to put Jesus to death but rather how. They wanted to be careful because many people believed in Jesus as the Messiah.

Verses 3–15 set the stage for events later in the chapter and require little explanation.

In verse 16, Jesus speaks of not eating the Passover again "until it is fulfilled in the kingdom of God." In verse 18, He speaks of not drinking of the fruit of the vine "until the kingdom of God comes." In both of these statements, He is speaking of the kingdom of God that will begin to come already with His death and resurrection and finally be consummated at His second coming. Jesus would share "new covenant" meals many times with His disciples, beginning with the meal at Emmaus.

So also, when the thief on the cross asked, "Jesus, remember me when You come into Your kingdom," Jesus said, "*Today* you will be with Me in Paradise" (Luke 23:42–43,

emphasis added). Thus, as Luther's Small Catechism explains, when we pray "Thy kingdom come," we are praying for a kingdom that *comes* to us (present tense) already today. This is all significant for understanding that, in verses 16 and 18, Jesus is predicting and promising His continuing fellowship with His Church in the Lord's Supper.

Luke is the only Gospel writer to mention two cups in his account of the Lord's Supper, one before the distribution of bread and one after (22:17, 20). This reflects Luke's more detailed account of the way the Passover meal was likely observed.

The more significant cup is the second one, which is mentioned also by the other evangelists and which Jesus refers to as "the new covenant in My blood" (v. 20). In light of the original Passover story (Exodus 12), one sees that this new meal involves the blood of Jesus as the *once-for-all* Passover Lamb. And it is a meal of a "new" covenant of grace and mercy sealed once for all by the death and resurrection of God's Son for the life of the world.

It is critical to emphasize the word *is*, which occurs twice in these verses: "This is My body" (v. 19); "This cup . . . is the new covenant in My blood" (v. 20). Though it is a mystery how this can be, we believe the clear word of Scripture that the word *is* truly means "is" and that the bread and wine of the Lord's Supper do not represent the body and blood of Jesus, but they truly *are* that body and blood.

To hear an in-depth discussion of this Bible account, visit cph.org/podcast and listen to our Seeds of Faith podcast each week.

Lesson 4
The Lord's Supper
Luke 22:1–23

Connections

Bible Words
[Jesus says,] "This is My blood . . . poured out for you . . . for the forgiveness of sins." Matthew 26:28

Faith Word
Lord's Supper

Hymn
Glory Be to Jesus (*LSB* 433; CD 2)

Catechism
Sacrament of the Altar

Liturgy
Holy Communion

Take-Home Point
Jesus gives forgiveness in the Lord's Supper.

1 Opening (15 minutes)

Welcome Time

What you do: Before class, set up two activity areas. In one, put out copies of Activity Page 4A and crayons. Make copies of Activity Page Fun (below and on CD) for parents or classroom helpers. Adjust talk as necessary.

In another area, cover a table with a plain paper tablecloth or large sheet of paper. Draw circle plates to make table settings. Make platters and bowls in the middle. Provide magazines with food pictures. Option: Set out play dough for the children to make food.

Play the CD from your Teacher Tools. As the children arrive, greet each one. Give them a sticker to put on the attendance chart.

Say Hi, [Everitt]. How are you? I wonder . . . what is your favorite food? Today we're going to learn about a special meal God gives us.

Direct child to one of the activities. Encourage parents or caregivers to do an activity with their child.

Activity Page Fun Get a copy of the Activity Page. Talk about the picture with your child as he or she colors and adds a favorite food to the table.

Say God gives us lots of good things to eat so we grow strong and healthy. Draw something you like to eat on the plate.

Today, you will hear about another special meal God gives us. It is called the Lord's Supper. Do you know what that is? Let child tell. Listen carefully today to find out what God gives us in this meal.

MATERIALS NEEDED

1 Opening	2 God Speaks	3 We Live	4 Closing
Teacher Tools Attendance chart CD	**Teacher Tools** Poster B	**Student Pack** Craft Page 4 Stickers	**Teacher Tools** CD
Student Pack Attendance sticker	**Student Pack** Lesson Leaflet 4 Stickers	**Other Supplies** Sprout or another puppet Bows or ribbon	**Student Pack** Take-home materials
Other Supplies Activity Page 4A (TG) Paper tablecloth or roll of paper Magazines Play dough Resource Page 1 (TG)	**Other Supplies** Memory game items, tray & towel Communion chalice & plate *The Very First Lord's Supper* Arch Book (optional)	Activity Pages 4B & 4C & Paper Plus supplies (optional) Grapes & vanilla wafers	

Active Learning Have the children tear out food pictures from magazines to glue to the plate and serving bowls you've drawn, or have them draw their favorite foods. *Option:* Have them make food out of play dough.

Ask **What is your favorite thing to eat?** Accept answers. **God gives us lots of good food! Today we will hear about a special meal He gives us called the Lord's Supper.**

Use your classroom signal to let the children know it's time to clean up and gather in your story area. Sing a cleanup song (Resource Page 1).

Sing **Come and listen to God's Word, to God's Word, to God's Word. Come and listen to God's Word from His book, the Bible.**

Gathering in God's Name

What you do: Begin with this opening. To teach about the Church Year, use the materials in the Church Year Worship Kit (see the introduction).

Sing "I'm in God's Family" (*S&W*, p. 58; CD 10) or "Glory Be to Jesus" (*LSB* 433; CD 2)

Say **I like to be in Sunday School with you, my friends! Today we'll learn about a special meal Jesus gives us.**

Invite the children to say the Invocation and Amen with you. Tell them "Amen" is the special word we say to ask Jesus to hear our prayers just like He promised.

Begin **In the name of the Father and of the Son and of the Holy Spirit. Amen.**

Offering Have a child bring the offering basket forward. Sing an offering song. Lead children in prayer, having them repeat after you at the asterisk. Tell them you will say a phrase and then they can pray it back to God.

Pray **Dear Jesus,* thank You* for loving us.* Thank You* for coming to earth* and dying on the cross to pay for our sins.* Help us remember* that You did this for us.* Amen.***

Celebrate Birthdays, Baptism birthdays, and special occasions

2 God Speaks (20 minutes)

Story Clue

What you do: Bring a cross, a baptismal shell or napkin, four or five small toys or household objects, a tray, and a towel for a memory game.

Play a memory game with the children. Have them name the items as you put them on the tray. Then cover the items with a towel.

Ask **Can you remember what I put on the tray?** Let the children say what they remember; then say, **Let's take off the towel and see if we remembered everything.** Touch and name each object. Touch the cross.

Ask **What is this?** Let children tell. **The cross helps us remember that Jesus died on a cross. He forgives our sin. We sin when we say and think and do wrong things.** Touch the shell.

Say This shell helps us remember our Baptism. Shells come from the water. When we were baptized, God washed away our sin and made us His children. You remembered the things on our tray so well! Play the game again. This time, ask the children to tell you what the cross and shell help us remember. **In our Bible story today, Jesus tells us to remember something too.**

Bible Story Time

What you do: Show Poster B as you tell the story. To begin, have your Bible open to the story and the poster facedown. Ask your pastor if you can borrow a Communion chalice and plate to show the children, or take pictures of these items on your tablet device or smartphone to show the children. *Option:* Read *The Very First Lord's Supper* Arch Book (CPH, 59-1501).

Say There is a special time in our church service when grown-ups and older children go to the front of the church for a special supper. Maybe you go with them. They stand or kneel at the Communion rail and eat bread and drink wine. If you go with them, you stand or kneel too, and the pastor gives you a special blessing from God. This special meal is called the Lord's Supper or Holy Communion. Jesus tells us in the Bible to do this to remember Him. Our Bible story today is about the time Jesus gave this meal to His disciples. Open your Bible.

It was almost time for Jesus to suffer and die on the cross to take away the sin of all people. Jesus knew He was going to die soon. He wanted to have one last supper with His twelve special friends, the disciples. So, Jesus told His friends to go to the house of a man He knew and tell him that Jesus and His friends wanted to use a room in the man's house. There, they could eat and visit by themselves.

Jesus was happy He could share a meal with His friends before He went away. After they ate, He did something special. He took some bread, gave thanks to God for it, and broke it into pieces. He gave a piece of it to each one of His friends and said, "Take, eat. This is My body, which is given for you. Eat this to remember Me." Show children the Communion plate for the bread.

Then Jesus took a cup of wine. Point to Jesus on Poster B. **He gave thanks to God for it and said, "Drink of it, all of you. This is My blood, which is poured out for you to take away your sins. Drink this to remember Me."** Show children a Communion chalice.

Jesus loved His friends. He loves us very much too. When we go to the Lord's Supper, Jesus forgives our sins. He reminds us that He loves us and will be with us always. Someday we will live with Him in our heavenly home.

Bible Story Review

What you do: Show Poster B to the class. Use the questions to review the story. Then hand out the leaflets, stickers, and crayons.

Ask **What are Jesus and His disciples doing?** Eating supper together

What is Jesus giving His disciples? Bread and wine

What is this special meal called? The Lord's Supper

Key Point

Jesus is our Passover Lamb, who with His very body and blood grants us forgiveness, life, and salvation.

Growing in CHRIST

What does Jesus do for us in the Lord's Supper? He forgives sins and strengthens faith.

Direct attention to the leaflet. On the sidebar, ask children to find the things pictured in the Bible story picture. They can draw something they remember about Jesus or from the story. Then do the activities on side 2 together. Give children stickers of a shell and cross. Point to the font.

Ask   **What is this? Let's color the water and add a shell sticker. In Baptism, God forgives our sins and makes us His children.** Point to the Bible. **What is this? We learn about Jesus in God's Word, the Bible. God tells us that He forgives our sins for Jesus' sake and helps us live as His children. Let's add a cross sticker to the Bible to show that.** Point to chalice and plate of bread. **What is this? Can you color the bread and wine? In the Lord's Supper, God forgives our sins and helps our faith grow.**

Bible Words

What you do: Read the Bible Words from Matthew 26:28 in the Bible.

Ask   **What special things did Jesus do to help His friends remember Him?** Let children tell to see what they learned from the Bible lesson; then clarify.

Say   **Jesus told His friends to eat the bread and drink the wine. He said, "This is My blood . . . poured out for you . . . for the forgiveness of sins." Jesus wanted His friends to remember that He loved them and forgave their sins. He wanted them to know He would be with them always.**

The Lord's Supper is a special and important time. In a wonderful way, we receive Jesus' true body with the bread and His true blood with the wine. In a wonderful way, Jesus forgives our sins and helps our faith to grow strong. Jesus is so good to us! Let's say our Bible Words now. Divide children into two groups to say the words. Then switch parts so they learn the verse.

Group 1: [Jesus says,] "This is My blood . . .

Group 2: poured out for you . . . for the forgiveness of sins."

 **3** **We Live** (20 minutes)

Help children grow in their understanding of what the Bible story means for their lives. Choose the activities that work best with your class.

Growing through God's Word

What you do: Bring out Sprout. Using puppets is therapeutic for children. They encourage language participation and interaction, especially for children who have visual, physical, or language delays.

Great Tip
for Special Need

Sprout: Hi, Teacher. I've been wondering about something. You said that Jesus wants us to go to the Lord's Supper to remember that He loves us. So, why can't the boys and girls eat the special supper from Jesus?

Teacher: They can, Sprout, and they will when they get older. But they have to learn more about Jesus and what He does for us first.

Sprout: Oh. So it's kind of like my neighbor Sammy. He's been taking swimming lessons every summer because he wants to be a lifeguard. He's a pretty good swimmer now, but he told me that he still has to take special lifeguard lessons to learn how to save people. And he can't take that class until he's fifteen! So he has to wait two more years before he can be a lifeguard.

Teacher: Yes, Sprout, it's kind of like that. Learning how to swim well enough to save people is very important. Eating the special supper Jesus gives us is very important too. When they get older, the boys and girls can go to Communion too, but not yet.

Sprout: What do they do now?

Teacher: Some boys and girls go to the front of the church when the grown-ups go to the Lord's Supper. When the pastor comes to the boy or girl, he makes the shape of a cross over him or her. *(Make sign of the cross over Sprout.)* The sign of the cross reminds the boy or girl of Baptism. At our Baptism, God makes us His children. He takes away our sins for Jesus' sake and promises we will live with Him in heaven.

Sprout: That's special. Would you make the sign of the cross for us all now?

Teacher: Sure, Sprout. When the pastor gives us God's blessing at the Communion rail and makes the sign of the cross over us, it is a wonderful reminder of God's love and forgiveness for us through His Son, Jesus. Boys and girls, why don't you make the sign of the cross with me as I say the blessing the pastor gives us at the altar? *(Demonstrate making the sign of the cross as you say the following.)* "Jesus loves you and died for your sins." You can make the sign of the cross whenever you want to remember God's love for you.

Sprout: Thanks, Teacher. Well, I gotta go to church now. See you next week!

Teacher: Bye, Sprout. *(Put Sprout down; address children.)* Boys and girls, I'm glad Sprout asked that question. I hope that the next time you go to the Lord's Supper, you remember that God loves you and made you His child in Baptism when He washed away your sins. Someday, you will get to eat His special Supper too. It is another way God forgives our sins and reminds us of His love in Jesus.

Craft Time

What you do: Give the children their Craft Pages, stickers, and crayons. Provide bows or ribbon to enhance the gift side of the project.

Begin with the hidden picture on the Craft Page, which shows two children in church receiving a blessing during Communion. Talk about what is happening in the picture.

Say In a wonderful way in the Lord's Supper, Jesus tells us that we receive His true body with the bread and His true blood with the wine. We cannot see them; they are hidden, but Jesus tells us they are there. This picture has some hidden Communion cups and bread. You can't see them right away either, but they are in the picture. Look carefully. How many can you find?

Give the children stickers of a chalice and bread to add to the hidden pictures they find. Help those who do not know what to look for. On the other side, have the children color the wine and bread and connect the dots to show a gift box. Have them color the ribbon, or give them a bow to add.

Directions

Use Activity Pages 4B and 4C to make a storybook scroll. You will also need a long strip of paper, two dowels, crayons, scissors, and tape or glue.

Color the figures and cut them out. Glue or tape them to the middle of a long strip of paper in the following order: Peter and John, man with a pitcher, the room, Jesus and disciples, Jesus and bread, Jesus and cup.

Attach a dowel to each end of the paper. Roll up the strip from both ends.

To tell the story, unroll the scroll to reveal the first picture. Roll left side closed; unroll right half to show next picture. Continue in this manner to tell the story.

4

Preparing the Lesson

Peter Denies Jesus

Mark 14:26–72

Key Point

Though we, like Peter, deny Jesus and His gifts, Jesus does not deny us because we belong to Him as baptized members of His Body, the Church. Instead, He forgives us and welcomes us back.

Law/**Gospel**

I deny Jesus when I fail to acknowledge Him and live as if I do not know Him. **Even when I deny Him, Jesus will never turn His back on me, never refuse me, and never stop loving me. Instead, He draws me back, forgives me, and treats me as if I had never denied Him.**

Context

It is Holy Thursday (also called Maundy Thursday). Having instituted the Lord's Supper, Jesus leads His disciples to the Mount of Olives, a familiar place to them. There, Peter refuses to believe what Jesus predicts: that he, along with the rest of the apostolic band, will desert and deny their Master. A few hours later, however, after Jesus is arrested and while He's being tried in the court of the Jews, Peter denies his Lord three times. Luke adds a detail skipped by the other evangelists, that at the third denial, "the Lord turned and looked at Peter" (22:61), calling to mind the prediction that Peter had fulfilled by his infidelity.

Commentary

Peter's pride went before his destruction, his haughty spirit before a most tragic fall (see Proverbs 16:18). Thinking he stood fast and strong, immovable in his devotion to Jesus, he did not heed his Lord's warning and prediction; thus, hard was his fall (see 1 Corinthians 10:12). That is what pride does. It is a sort of self-created devil within each of us, by which we deceive ourselves into thinking that we are impregnable.

We suppose that we are stronger than our peers, that though "all fall away, I will not" (Mark 14:29). Like Peter, we think that though our comrades succumb to temptation, we will not; though the whole world go to hell in a hand-basket, we will remain steady on our feet, eyes unblinking, a gold medal around our neck. Pride is the first and ultimate self-deception, for by it, we paint a self-portrait in which our face shines with more than a hint of divinity.

But when tears stained the countenance of Peter's own prideful self-portrait, he came to the painful realization that he was no better than his friends, indeed, no better than the scoundrels who at that moment were railroading Jesus to the cross and grave. In his three denials, Peter not only stabbed Jesus in the back, but he also sank the knife into his own soul. Indeed, he denounced the very One to whom he had pledged unflinching loyalty.

Our own denials of Jesus may not be as dramatic, but they are just as real. Whether by speaking or by keeping silent when we ought to speak up, we have all chosen love of self over love of Savior. We have denied our Lord and His gifts for the sake of reputation or some other selfish gain. And the rooster's crow has called us all to repentance.

Jesus, however, never denies us. He forgives Peter's threefold denial and welcomes Him back with His three-fold question: "Simon, son of John, do you love Me?" (John 21:15–17). Even if we are faithless, He remains faithful. He cannot deny us because we are part of Him, baptized members of His Body.

To hear an in-depth discussion of this Bible account, visit cph.org/podcast and listen to our Seeds of Faith podcast each week.

Lesson 5

Peter Denies Jesus

Mark 14:26–72

Connections

Bible Words
If we are faithless, [Jesus] remains faithful. 2 Timothy 2:13

Faith Word
Repent

Hymn
Glory Be to Jesus (*LSB* 433; CD 2)

Catechism
Apostles' Creed: Second Article

Liturgy
Confession and Absolution

Take-Home Point
Jesus loves me all the time.

1 Opening (15 minutes)

Welcome Time

What you do: Before class, set up two activity areas. In one, put out copies of Activity Page 5A and crayons. Make copies of Activity Page Fun (below and on CD) for parents or classroom helpers. Adjust talk as necessary.

In another area, set out play dough and cross cookie cutters.

Play the CD from your Teacher Tools. As the children arrive, greet each one. Give them a sticker to put on the attendance chart.

Say Hi, [Teigen]. It's good to see you! I wonder . . . how was your week? Today we'll hear about something that happened during the week Jesus died for us.

Direct child to one of the activities. Encourage parents or caregivers to do an activity with their child.

Activity Page Fun Get a copy of the Activity Page. Point to *yes* and *no*.

Ask What do these two words say? Let child tell. **Can you trace the lines of each mouth? What do you see?**

Say The "yes" has a face with a smile. The "no" has a face with a frown. Have child trace the words and finish the faces. **Your Bible story today is about Peter and some questions he had trouble answering.**

MATERIALS NEEDED

1 Opening	2 God Speaks	3 We Live	4 Closing
Teacher Tools Attendance chart CD	**Teacher Tools** CD	**Student Pack** Craft Page 5 Stickers	**Teacher Tools** CD
Student Pack Attendance sticker	**Student Pack** Lesson Leaflet 5	**Other Supplies** Sprout or other puppet Paper fasteners (brads) Activity Page 5B & Paper Plus supplies (optional) Heart-shaped cookies	**Student Pack** Take-home items
Other Supplies Activity Page 5A (TG) Play dough & cross cookie cutters Resource Page 1 (TG)	**Other Supplies** *Yes* and *no* cards (Activity Page 5A, TG) *The Night Peter Cried* Arch Book (optional)		

Active Learning Show children how to make crosses using cookie cutters or by rolling play dough into ropes.

Say **Crosses remind us that Jesus forgives us. Let's make a cross over ourselves.** Make the sign of the cross. **Jesus forgives sins. In our story today, we will hear how Peter sinned. I wonder . . . did Jesus forgave him?**

Option: Play a yes-or-no game with the children, asking them questions in a group that require the same answer from all of them (e.g., "Is it raining?" or "Am I wearing a black skirt?"). Very young children can become confused when their answer isn't the same as everyone else's.

Use your classroom signal to let the children know it's time to clean up and gather in your story area. Sing a cleanup song (Resource Page 1).

Gathering in God's Name

What you do: Begin with this opening. To teach about the Church Year, use the materials in the Church Year Worship Kit (see the introduction).

Sing "I'm in God's Family" (*S&W*, p. 58; CD 10) or "Glory Be to Jesus" (*LSB* 433; CD 2)

Invite the children to say the Invocation and Amen with you. Tell them "Amen" is the special word we say to ask Jesus to hear our prayers just like He promised.

Begin **In the name of the Father and of the Son and of the Holy Spirit. Amen.**

Offering Have a child bring the offering basket forward. Sing an offering song.

Pray **Dear Jesus, thank You for loving us. No matter what we do, You still love us and promise to forgive us. You are our Savior. Amen.**

Celebrate Birthdays, Baptism birthdays, and special occasions

2 God Speaks (20 minutes)

Story Clue

What you do: Have the children use the cards that you made from Activity Page 5A for Welcome Time, or prepare the *yes* and *no* cards to use now. Instead of having the children hold up their cards, show the card you made to prompt their answers.

Say **I'm going to ask you some questions. You can answer my questions by saying yes or no and holding up the *yes* or *no* card you made to answer the question.** Hold up the smiley face for *yes* and the frowning face for *no*.

Ask **Does Jesus love us?** Hold up the *yes* card. **Yes, He does.**
Do we love Jesus? Hold up the *yes* card. **Yes, we do.**
Do we always do everything Jesus tells us to do? Hold up the *no* card. **No, we don't.**
Our story today tells us about some questions that Peter answered. Do you think Peter said yes or no? Let's listen and find out.

Bible Story Time

What you do: Use the yes-or-no cards as you listen to the story on track 20 of the CD, or tell it using the script below. *Option:* Tell the story using the Arch Book *The Night Peter Cried* (CPH, 59-2284).

Say **Jesus was praying in the Garden of Gethsemane. His disciples were there, but they were sleeping. Jesus knew that it was almost time for Him to die on the cross. Suddenly, some soldiers came to arrest Jesus. March, march, march.** March in place. **Jesus' disciples were afraid. They ran away because they did not want the soldiers to catch them too.**

The enemy soldiers took Jesus out of the garden. March in place. **Peter decided to follow them, but he stayed far behind because he did not want the soldiers to see him. The soldiers took Jesus to the house of the high priest. Peter stayed outside in the courtyard. There were many servants and guards working there. They had built a fire to keep warm. Peter walked over to the fire to warm up.** Extend hands over pretend fire.

Soon, a servant girl saw him. She asked, "Aren't you one of Jesus' disciples?" Peter was one of Jesus' disciples. He should have said yes. Coach children to hold up the *yes* card. **But Peter was afraid. He did not want them to know he was Jesus' friend. He worried that they would arrest him too. So Peter said, "No, I don't know Him."** Hold up *no* card.

Then, Peter walked over to the gate. The servant girl saw him again. She told the guards, "That man was with Jesus. He is one of His followers." Peter should have said yes, he was. Hold up *yes* card. **But Peter was still afraid. So, he said, "No, I'm not."** Hold up *no* card.

After a while, some guards walked over to Peter. They said, "You must be one of Jesus' friends. You even talk like Him." Peter should have said yes. Hold up *yes* card. **But Peter was still afraid. He lied a third time. He shouted, "No, I do not know that man!"** Hold up *no* card.

Just then, a rooster crowed. Peter remembered what Jesus had told him before they went to the garden to pray: "Before the rooster crows twice, you will say three times that you do not know Me." Now Peter was sad. He left the courtyard of the house and began to cry. He was sorry because he knew he had hurt Jesus. He knew he had sinned.

Did Jesus still love Peter? Yes, Jesus still loved Peter. Hold up *yes* card. **Did Jesus forgive Peter?** Hold up *yes* card. **Yes, Jesus forgave Peter. Does Jesus forgive us?** Hold up *yes* card. **Yes, Jesus forgives us too.**

Sometimes, we act like we don't know Jesus. We do this when we sin. Maybe we are mean to our friends. Maybe we disobey our parents. Maybe we don't pay attention in church. Maybe we do things we know God doesn't want us to do. These are all sins.

But Jesus died on the cross to pay for all our sins. He makes us His children through Baptism and His Word. He forgives us when we do wrong things. Jesus never says, "No, I don't know you." Show *no* card.

He always says, "Yes, I love you. Yes, you are My child. Yes, I forgive you." Hold up *yes* card each time. **Thank You, Jesus, for loving us, no matter what.**

Key Point

Though we, like Peter, deny Jesus and His gifts, Jesus does not deny us because we belong to Him as baptized members of His Body, the Church. Instead, He forgives us and welcomes us back.

Growing in CHRIST

Bible Story Review

What you do: Show Lesson Leaflet 5 as you use the questions to review. Play a game; then hand out the leaflets and crayons.

Ask **Where is Peter?** He is in the courtyard of the high priest.

Does Peter tell the truth when the servants ask if he knows Jesus? No.

How does Peter look? Sad, sorry for sinning

Will Jesus forgive Peter? Yes.

Play a version of Mother, May I? For each *yes* question, have the children jump forward one jump. For each *no*, the children stand still. If the children made the yes-or-no cards, they can hold those up instead. Use questions such as the following.

Ask **Did the servant girl ask Peter if he knew Jesus?** Yes.
Did Peter tell her that he did? No.
Did Peter tell anyone that he knew Jesus before the rooster crowed? No.
Did Peter cry and feel sorry about his sin? Yes.
Did Jesus forgive him? Yes.
Does Jesus forgive you when you sin? Yes.

Hand out the leaflets and talk about the activity on the back.

Say **These children have done something naughty. Who loves us no matter how much we sin? Yes, Jesus does! Draw a cross over the children to show that Jesus will forgive them.**

Bible Words

What you do: Read 2 Timothy 2:13 from your Bible: "If we are faithless, [Jesus] remains faithful." Divide children into two groups to say the words. Switch parts and say them again.

Say **Our Bible Words are from 2 Timothy 2:13: "If we are faithless, [Jesus] remains faithful." Let's think about what this means.**

Peter was scared. When people asked if he knew Jesus, he said no. Peter was faithless. Hold up *no* card. **He pretended not to know Jesus. He sinned. But Jesus is faithful.** Hold up *yes* card. **He did not forget about Peter. He kept on loving him. He forgave Peter.**

Sometimes we are afraid too. We don't trust Jesus to care for us. Sometimes we do wrong things. We sin. We are faithless too. Hold up *no* card. **But Jesus is always faithful.** Hold up *yes* card. **Jesus showed how much He loved Peter and all of us by going to the cross to pay for our sins. He will always love us, no matter what. Let's say our Bible Words.**

Group 1: If we are faithless, *Hold up* no *cards.*

Group 2: [Jesus] remains faithful. *Hold up* yes *cards.*

Teacher Tip

Young children are just becoming aware of the feelings and needs of others. When problems occur in the classroom, talk about actions and the effect they have on others. Do not force insincere apologies, but do pray for God's help to forgive.

3 We Live (20 minutes)

Help children grow in their understanding of what the Bible story means for their lives. Choose the activities that work best with your class.

Growing through God's Word

What you do: You will need Sprout and a heart-with-cross sticker from each child's Sticker Page. *Option:* Create a puppet show of this dialogue using the "Sock Puppets" app available for iPhone, iPod Touch, or iPad. Search "sock puppet app" online for how to download the app and create the puppet play.

Teacher: How are you today, Sprout?

Sprout: I'm fine. I was thinking about the questions in our story. I would never say I didn't know Jesus. I know who Jesus is!

Teacher: Well, Sprout, all of us act like we don't know Jesus at times.

Sprout: What do you mean?

Teacher: Well, have you ever said something mean about someone? Have you ever hit someone or disobeyed? Have you ever not wanted to go to church?

Sprout: *(Hanging head)* Yeah . . . I guess so.

Teacher: Well, Sprout, those things are all sins. Sin is not doing what God wants us to do. When God's children do things like that, we are forgetting about God and how He wants us to live. We are sinning just as Peter did.

Sprout: What do we do then?

Teacher: We can repent. That means we can tell God we are sorry for our sins and ask God to forgive us. And you know what? Jesus came to take our punishment on the cross for all our sins. Because of Jesus, God does forgive all our sins! He is so good to us. *(Show sticker of heart with a cross.)* This sticker of a heart with a cross on it will help us remember that God loved us so much that He sent Jesus to die on the cross for all of us. Can you help me give one to the boys and girls, Sprout? *(Give each child the sticker to wear.)*

Sprout: God is so good to us. Can we sing "God Is So Good" (*LOSP*, p. 57)? (*Do so.*)

Craft Time

What you do: Give each child a copy of Craft Page 5, stickers, crayons or markers, and paper fasteners (brads). Cut off the strip with the arrow and the heart.

Note: Some children will need extra time to complete the craft. Break the directions into manageable steps and give help as needed.

Say **Jesus loves us all the time. When other people aren't kind to us, or when we have done wrong, Jesus still loves us. Even when people act like they don't love us or when we act like we don't love other people, Jesus promises to keep loving us. Let's make a picture to show all the times Jesus loves us.** Help children cut out and attach the strip with the heart to the center of the circle using a paper fastener. Give them heart stickers with Jesus' face to add to the dotted hearts.

Say **When you attach the arrow to your picture, you can show all the times that Jesus loves us. In the first picture, the little boy is asleep. Jesus loves him. In the next picture, the little girl and her mom are taking their dog for a walk. Jesus loves them. In the next picture, the little boy is playing with a friend. Jesus loves him. In the last picture, the little boy and girl are angry with each other. They are fighting. Jesus still loves them. Put the Jesus stickers next to all the pictures.**

Give the children ribbon, yarn, and stickers of hearts, Jesus, and a Bible for the rebus on side 2. Have children color the flowers and the child's face to look like theirs. Talk about how Jesus loves and forgives us, no matter what.

Paper Plus option: Make a "Jesus Loves Me" hanging. Enlarge and copy Jesus' face on Activity Page 5B for each child. Help children do these steps: Color and cut out Jesus' face. Glue it to a paper plate. Draw hearts and crosses or add purchased heart and cross stickers to the rim. Write "Jesus loves me" on the bottom of the rim. (See finished craft on top of the page.) Punch a hole in the top of the plate and string with yarn for hanging. *Option:* For younger children, enlarge and copy Jesus' face on top of the Activity Page. Have them color it, cut it out, and glue to a paper plate.

Snack Time

What you do: Serve heart-shaped cookies with a frosting cross. Remind the children of God's love for us. He never forgets about us.

Live It Out

What you do: Talk about the Confession and Absolution in worship. Lead children in an "I am sorry" prayer; then, sing the following to the tune of "Praise Him, Praise Him" (*LOSP*, p. 68).

Sing **Pray to Jesus, all you little children.**
He forgives, He forgives.
Pray to Jesus, all you little children.
He forgives, He forgives.

4 Closing (5 minutes)

Going Home

What you do: Send home take-home items and crafts. Cue CD.

Say **Peter sinned when he lied. But Jesus forgave him. We sin too. But Jesus loves us all the time. He helps us to be sorry for our sins. He forgives us. Let's say, "Jesus loves me all the time" together.** Do so.

Sing "Jesus Loves Me" (*LOSP*, p. 42; CD 14)

Pray After each petition, have the children respond, "Jesus, we are sorry. Please forgive us."

Dear Jesus, sometimes, we fight with a friend.
Children: Jesus, we are sorry. Please forgive us.
Sometimes, we don't do what our mom or dad says.
Children respond. Continue with several other petitions.
Conclude, **Thank You, Jesus, for dying on the cross to take away our sins. Thank You for Your love and forgiveness. Amen.**

Reflection

Did the children understand that when we don't talk and act like Jesus' children, we are sinning? More important, did they understand that Jesus continues to love and forgive them, no matter what?

Trace the words and finish the faces.

Yes

Add a smile.

No

Add a frown.

Preparing the Lesson

The Passion of Christ

Matthew 27:11–66

Key Point

The Father, the perfect, righteous judge of the universe, gave His Son, Jesus, as the perfect, righteous sacrifice on the cross and punished Him for the sin of the whole world.

Law/**Gospel**

The wages of sin is death. **Jesus Christ paid the price for the sin of the world by His suffering and death.**

Context

It had been only a few hours since Jesus had celebrated the Last Supper with His disciples, after which Judas betrayed Him into the hands of the Jewish religious leaders (Matthew 26:47–50). Jesus then stood trial before the Jewish leaders, where He was charged with blasphemy—that is, claiming to be God (vv. 64–66).

The Jews punished blasphemy with death, but under Roman rule, the Jews did not have authority to execute anyone. Thus, Jesus was sent before Pontius Pilate, the Roman governor, to be sentenced. Pilate seemed to want to be fair in his judgment (27:11–14, 18, 23), but ultimately he succumbed to the pressure of the crowd and his desire to keep the peace (v. 24). (Note: Much of the detail for the painting in today's lesson is based on the account in John 19.)

In Roman crucifixion, the executing soldiers took the criminal's belongings as spoil (Matthew 27:35). A victim of crucifixion had his feet nailed high enough that his body would be slightly slumped, making breathing difficult. He would probably die of suffocation. Other causes of death were dehydration or—especially for victims who were scourged, as was Jesus (v. 26)—loss of blood.

Commentary

Righteousness is an important concept throughout Matthew's Gospel. Jesus begins His ministry by being baptized to "fulfill all righteousness" (3:15). He calls people to

be perfect, as their heavenly Father is perfect (5:48). In His Passion, Jesus completes what He began at His Baptism: fulfilling all righteousness, which we could not do. We can see the importance of the Passion in the length and detail of Matthew's account (26:36–27:66). The tension of how sinners can be made righteous climaxes in this suffering of Christ and is resolved in Christ's resurrection from the dead.

Although Jesus is condemned for blasphemy, He is the one man who can truly claim to be God. Thus, He is falsely accused, while around Him other men go unpunished for betrayal (26:47–50), denial (26:69–75), false testimony (26:59–61), envy (27:18), cowardice (27:24), mockery (27:39–44), and murder (27:26, 35).

In the same way, Jesus is falsely accused for our crimes, but He takes our punishment in love so that we may walk away completely free. The Father forsakes Jesus—an event that is incomprehensible to us—so that the sin of the whole world is punished by the perfect, righteous judge of the universe through the perfect, righteous sacrifice, Jesus Christ.

Like the centurion, we see at the cross who Christ really is: the Righteous One who makes us righteous (27:54). For His sake, God does not hold our sins against us; neither does He maintain His demands forever upon us. God takes up our sins, demands, burdens, and sufferings so that, forgiven and clean, we rise to new life.

To hear an in-depth discussion of this Bible account, visit cph.org/podcast and listen to our Seeds of Faith podcast each week.

Lesson 6

The Passion of Christ

Matthew 27:11–66

Connections

Bible Words
In [Jesus] we have . . .
the forgiveness of sins.
Colossians 1:14

Faith Word
Hosanna

Hymn
Glory Be to Jesus (*LSB* 433;
CD 2)

Catechism
Apostles' Creed:
Second Article

Take-Home Point
Jesus takes away my sins.

1 Opening (15 minutes)

Welcome Time

What you do: Before class, set up two activity areas. In one, put out copies of Activity Page 6 and crayons. Make copies of Activity Page Fun (below and on CD) for parents or classroom helpers. Adjust talk as necessary.

In another area, set out play dough, cross cookie cutters, and circles cut out of construction paper.

Play the CD from your Teacher Tools. As the children arrive, greet each one. Give them a sticker to put on the attendance chart.

Say Hi, [Jarek]. How are you? I wonder . . . what does a cross remind you of? Today we'll hear about how Jesus died on the cross for us.

Direct child to one of the activities. Encourage parents or caregivers to do an activity with their child.

Activity Page Fun Get a copy of the Activity Page. Ask your child to look at each box and decide if this is something God wants us to do or if it is a sin—something God does not want us to do. (Define *sin* as needed.)

Say If you think the picture shows something God wants us to do, color it. If the picture shows something God doesn't want us to do—a sin—put a big X on it. Help your child decide what the picture shows, and color it together. Then continue. **We all do wrong things, things that God does not want us to say or do. But God loves us very much and sent Jesus to be our Savior. Today, you will hear how Jesus saved us from our sins.**

MATERIALS NEEDED

1 Opening	2 God Speaks	3 We Live	4 Closing
Teacher Tools Attendance chart CD	**Teacher Tools** CD	**Student Pack** Craft Page 6 Stickers	**Teacher Tools** CD
Student Pack Attendance sticker	**Student Pack** Lesson Leaflet 6 Stickers	**Other Supplies** Sprout or another puppet with backpack	**Student Pack** Take-home items
Other Supplies Activity Page 6 (TG) Play dough Cross cookie cutters Construction paper circles Resource Page 1 (TG)	**Other Supplies** Props & story bag (optional) Picture of Garden of Gethsemane *The Week That Led to Easter* Arch Book (optional)	Prepared piece of paper Paper fasteners Paper Plus supplies (optional) Apple slices & fruit dip	

Active Learning Give the children play dough and cross cookie cutters to use. Cut circles out of construction paper, and have the children make happy and sad faces by adding play-dough eyes and mouths. Tell them that today they will hear about something that is both sad and happy.

Use your classroom signal to let the children know it's time to clean up and gather in your story area. Sing a cleanup song (Resource Page 1).

Gathering in God's Name

What you do: Begin with this opening. To teach about the Church Year, use the materials in the Church Year Worship Kit (see the introduction).

Say **Hi, boys and girls! I'm glad you are here to learn about our Friend and Savior, Jesus. Let's sing a song about the things Jesus did the week He died on the cross for us. We will talk more about that today.**

Sing "Jesus in Jerusalem" (*S&W*, p. 38; CD 13). If desired, also sing "Glory Be to Jesus" (*LSB* 433; CD 2).

Invite the children to say the Invocation and Amen with you. Tell them "Amen" is the special word we say to ask Jesus to hear our prayers just like He promised.

Begin **In the name of the Father and of the Son and of the Holy Spirit. Amen.**

Offering Have a child bring the offering basket forward. Sing an offering song.

Pray **Dear God,* please forgive our sins.***
Help us to listen.* Help us learn* more about You.* Amen.*
*Use the echo prayer format.

Celebrate Birthdays, Baptism birthdays, and special occasions

2 God Speaks (20 minutes)

Story Clue

What you do: Pantomime the following ideas. If you wish, put a prop in your story bag and show it as you act out each situation (e.g., birthday candles, an ornament, blanket to sit on or picnic basket).

Say **I'm going to act out some things that make us feel happy. See if you can guess what they are.** Pantomime the following things:

A birthday *Unwrap gifts, blow out candles, etc.*
Christmas *Hang ornaments, give gifts.*
A picnic *Carry picnic basket, put out blanket, peek in basket for food, etc.*

Say **Those were great guesses, children. Jesus makes us happy too, doesn't He? He is our best Friend and Savior.**

Ask **What happened on Easter?** Accept answers.

Say **Easter is a happy time! It is the day Jesus came back to life. But something sad had to happen before we could have a happy Easter Day. Let's listen to the Bible story and find out what sad thing happened.**

Teacher Tip
Having a routine each week may get old for adults, but young children find comfort in routines and rituals. This is especially true for children with special needs.

Bible Story Time

What you do: Listen to the story on track 21 of the CD, or tell the story using the following script. Ask the children to join you in doing the motions. Have your Bible open to Matthew 27:11–66, and point to where the Bible story is written to show the children they are hearing God's Word.

Ahead of time, search the Internet for a picture of the Garden of Gethsemane and print it to show the children, or show them a picture of the garden on your iPad or smartphone. Show picture on leaflet where indicated. *Option:* Read the story from the Arch Book *The Week That Led to Easter* (CPH, 59-1541).

Say **Jesus knew that it would soon be time for Him to suffer and die for us. So, He took His friends to a quiet place to pray. This place was called the Garden of Gethsemane.** Show picture of Garden of Gethsemane.

Jesus prayed and asked His Father in heaven to make Him strong for what He had to do. While Jesus was praying (fold hands), **some soldiers came to take Jesus away. Left foot, right foot, left foot, right foot, marched the soldiers.** Step in place. **They took Jesus to the house of some important church rulers.**

Some men were there who told lies about Jesus. They said Jesus did bad things. The leader of the church rulers asked Jesus, "Are You God's Son?"

Jesus answered, "Yes." That made the church leader angry. He shouted, "You are lying!" He and the others did not believe that Jesus was God's Son. They said Jesus should be put to death. They spit on Jesus and hit Him. But Jesus did not say anything. He did not fight back.

The next morning, they took Jesus to the ruler of the country. This man's name was Pilate (PIE lat). Show picture on leaflet. **Pilate asked, "What has Jesus done wrong?" The church rulers told Pilate, "Jesus is a troublemaker. He thinks He is a king!"** Place hands on head like a crown.

Pilate did not think Jesus had done anything wrong. He did not want to hurt Jesus. So Pilate thought of an idea. Point to head. **There was a man in jail who had done really bad things. This man's name was Barabbas (buh RAB bas). Pilate went outside and asked the people, "Do you want me to set Barabbas free, or should I let Jesus go?"**

The people shouted, "Free Barabbas!" Pilate was surprised. He asked, "What do you want me to do with Jesus?" The people shouted, "Nail Jesus to a cross!"

Pilate told his soldiers to take Jesus away. Remove picture. **Left foot, right foot, left foot, right foot, marched the solders.** Step in place. **The soldiers dressed Jesus in a robe and gave Him a stick. They put a crown made out of prickly thorns on Jesus' head. Then they pretended Jesus was a king. They said mean things to Him and hit Him. Jesus let the soldiers hurt Him. He did not say anything.**

Finally, the soldiers took Jesus to a hill outside the city. Left foot, right foot, left foot, right foot, marched the soldiers. The soldiers put Jesus on a cross. Draw cross in air with finger. **It hurt Jesus very much. But Jesus stayed on the cross so that He could take the punishment for our sins. He asked God to forgive those who hurt Him.**

Jesus' friends and His mother were there too. They were sad and cried.

Key Point

The Father, the perfect, righteous judge of the universe, gave His Son, Jesus, as the perfect, righteous sacrifice on the cross and punished Him for the sin of the whole world.

Growing in CHRiST

Make sad face. **Finally, the sky grew dark. The earth shook. Jesus cried out with a loud voice, "It is finished." Then He died.**

A man named Joseph and some of Jesus' friends took Jesus' body off the cross. They put Him in a tomb—a cave in the side of a hill. Then they rolled a big stone in front of the door. Pretend to push stone. **Slowly, slowly** (step in place)**, Jesus' friends left the tomb and went home.**

After that, Pilate sent soldiers to Jesus' tomb. Left foot, right foot, left foot, right foot, marched the soldiers. The soldiers guarded the place where Jesus was buried so no one would steal His body.

Jesus' friends were very sad the day Jesus suffered and died on the cross. But they didn't have to be sad for long. We know that Jesus did not stay dead. On Easter morning, He came alive again!

Jesus showed how much He loves us. He suffered and died and rose again so that our sins would be forgiven. Because He did this and we believe in Him, we can live with Him in heaven someday. What a happy ending to this sad story!

Bible Story Review

What you do: You need Lesson Leaflet 6, crayons, and stickers. Show the picture on the leaflet.

Ask **What did the people tell Pilate to do with Jesus?** Put Him on a cross

For whom did Jesus die? Everyone

What is the happy ending to this true story? Jesus came alive again on Easter.

How much does Jesus love you? Jesus loves us so much that He died to pay for our sins. He promises to take all those who believe in Him to heaven.

Hand out the leaflets. Draw attention to the pictures in the side box. Have children find matching faces in the Bible art, and give them stickers to add.

On side 2, have children color the stained glass window.

Option: Teach the children sign language for "Jesus died for me":

Say **Jesus**   *Touch center of each palm.*
        died   *Make cross with forearms.*
        for me   *Point to self.*

Practice the sentence with actions a few times; then, do this action rhyme with the children. Have them use sign language with their refrain.

Say **On the cross upon a hill,**   Children: Jesus died for me.
        With enemies and soldiers laughing,   Children: Jesus died for me.
        All according to God's plan,   Children: Jesus died for me.
        To take away all my sins,   Children: Jesus died for me.
        Amen.

Bible Words

What you do: Have your Bible open to Colossians 1:14: "In [Jesus] we have . . . the forgiveness of sins."

Say **As I say each thing, show me a thumbs-up if it is happy or thumbs-down if it is sad.**

Say Soldiers arrested Jesus. *Thumbs down*
Some people lied and said Jesus was a troublemaker. *Thumbs down*
Soldiers nailed Jesus to a cross. *Thumbs down*
All of those were very sad things.

Now listen to our Bible Words, and show me a thumbs-up or thumbs-down.

[In Jesus] we have . . . the forgiveness of sins. *Thumbs up*
This is the happy news! Today, we heard how Jesus died on the cross for us. But Jesus did not stay dead. On Easter, He came back to life!

Because Jesus died and rose again for us, God forgives our sins. Someday, we will have a beautiful home in heaven with Him. That is happy news too! *Thumbs up*

Have the children say the Bible Words with you again. If you wish, divide them into two groups. Have the first group say the first half and the second group say the ending. Switch and say the words again.

③ We Live (20 minutes)

Help children grow in their understanding of what the Bible story means for their lives. Choose the activities that work best with your class.

Growing through God's Word

What you do: You will need Sprout with his backpack. Have a piece of paper with a list of things to do titled "My Plan" sticking out of his backpack.

Teacher: Children, can you say hi to Sprout? *(Children say "Hi.")*

Sprout: Hi, everyone.

Teacher: Sprout, you have something sticking out of your backpack. *(Take out paper.)* What is this?

Sprout: Oh, that's my plan.

Teacher: Your plan?

Sprout: I was having a problem with my room. It is way too messy. So I made a plan to help me keep it neat.

Teacher: A plan is a super idea, Sprout.

Sprout: Thanks, Teacher. Well, I better go and start working on my messy room. Good-bye, everyone. *(Children wave and say "Bye.")*

Say **In our Bible story today, we heard how Jesus suffered and died on a cross for you and me. It makes us sad to think about how much our sins hurt Jesus. But it was all part of God's plan for Jesus to do this.**

God sent Jesus to earth to be our Savior. Jesus loves us so much that He let Himself be punished for us. Jesus even died for us. Because Jesus did this, God forgives our sins. Now, everyone who believes in Jesus can go to heaven and live with Him forever.

Craft Time

What you do: You will need Craft Page 6, scissors, paper fasteners (brads),

Growing in CHRIST.

crayons, and stickers to make a story wheel for retelling the Bible story.

Have children color the four Bible-story scenes on the yellow circle. Then, help them cut out the purple and yellow circles and cut out the pie-shaped wedge on the purple circle.

Put the purple circle with the sticker outlines showing on top of the Bible story scenes. Fasten the circles together near the center with a brad. The purple circle will spin, revealing the story scenes in the pie-shaped opening.

Give children the stickers to place on the shapes on the purple circle. Have them draw a picture of themselves in the face shape and write their name on the blank line on this circle. On the yellow circle, have them trace the letters in Jesus and write their name on the line. Demonstrate how to turn the wheel and tell the story. Practice reading the sentence: "Jesus died for [name]!"

Paper Plus option: Make stained glass crosses. Cover the work area with newspaper. Give each child a large cross cut from white paper. Have children color their crosses. Rub the *back* of each cross with cooking oil so it becomes translucent. When the cross dries, cut out a frame for it from construction paper. Hang in a sunlit window.

Snack Time

What you do: Serve apple slices and fruit dip. Turn the apple slices upside down. Discuss how they look like sad mouths. Our sin, the things we think and say and do wrong, makes God and others sad. But Jesus died on the cross and rose again to pay for our sins. Turn apple slices to look like smiles. That makes us happy.

Live It Out

What you do: Encourage children to show their craft to a friend or family member and tell that person how Jesus died and rose again for us.

Faith in Action!

4 Closing (5 minutes)

Going Home

What you do: Send take-home pages and crafts home with the children. Have CD player and CD cued to play.

Sing   "Do You Know Who Died for Me?" (*LOSP*, p. 93; CD 8)

Say   **Today, we heard about God's plan to take away our sin. He sent Jesus to be our Savior. Jesus loved us so much that He died on the cross and rose again to take away our sins.** Say "Jesus takes away my sin" together.

Pray   **Dear Jesus, it makes us sad when we hear about Your suffering and death on the cross. But we are happy that You rose again on Easter. We are happy that You took away our sins! Thank You for loving us. Amen.**

Reflection

Ask yourself, "How did I handle the wiggly, unfocused children? Did I still model God's love to them?"

Color the things God wants us to do. Put an X over things that God doesn't want us to do.

Preparing the Lesson

Date of Use

The Resurrection of Jesus

Matthew 28:1–10

Key Point

The resurrection reveals that the Father has accepted the Son's sacrifice for our sins, and it fills us with confident hope that, as Christ has been raised from the dead, we, too, will rise to eternal life.

Law/**Gospel**

Because of sin, I deserve eternal death and separation from God, and I am filled with fear. **The Father has accepted His Son's sacrifice for sin, making me an heir of eternal life. He works through His Word to comfort me, replacing my fear with joy and empowering me to tell others about the Lord's resurrection.**

Context

The events of this day stand at the center of salvation history. The resurrection is the foundation of our faith. Matthew mentions two of the women at the tomb on Easter: Mary Magdalene and the "other Mary." This Mary is the wife of Clopas and the sister of Mary, the mother of our Lord (John 19:25). At dawn on Sunday morning, the women approached the tomb to anoint the body of Jesus.

Commentary

When Jesus died on Good Friday, there was an earthquake. The tombs of many believers broke open, and they were raised to life (Matthew 27:52). On Easter, there was another earthquake as the angel came down from heaven and rolled the stone away to reveal that Jesus was alive (28:2). Earthquakes in Scripture often denote God's intervention in this world and reveal His might and glory (Exodus 19:18; 1 Kings 19:11; Acts 4:31; 16:26).

The angel at the tomb reinforces the significance of this event. Angels often proclaim important events in salvation history. In the events surrounding the first Christmas, angels appeared to Zechariah, Mary, Joseph, and the shepherds. Now at the resurrection, the angel proclaims that Christ has risen.

The guards watching the tomb, and later the women, were afraid of the angel. However, the women had no need to fear, for the angel's message was one of good news. The resurrection Gospel is ultimately what alleviates all fear as our Lord promises to forgive and help us, now and forever.

When Jesus met the women, they worshiped Him. Worship is reserved for God alone. By bowing down before Him, these women revealed their faith in Jesus as the Son of God. Worship is also our response as, in the Divine Service, we hear the Easter message and respond with our praise and adoration.

"If Christ has not been raised, your faith is futile and you are still in your sins" (1 Corinthians 15:17). The resurrection shows that Jesus is the Son of God and that His Word is true. It is just "as He said" (Matthew 28:6). The resurrection also reveals that the Father accepted the Son's sacrifice for our sins. The resurrection fills us with hope, for we know that as Christ has been raised from the dead, we, too, will rise to eternal life. In Baptism, we were joined to the death and resurrection of Christ, and since we have been united with Him in a death like His, we will certainly be united with Him in a resurrection like His (Romans 6:3–11).

To hear an in-depth discussion of this Bible account, visit cph.org/podcast and listen to our Seeds of Faith podcast each week.

Lesson 7

The Resurrection of Jesus
Matthew 28:1–10

Connections

Bible Words
[The angel said,] "He is not here, for He has risen, as He said." Matthew 28:6 (CD 4)

Faith Word
Alleluia

Hymn
Jesus Christ Is Risen Today (*LSB* 457; CD 3)

Catechism
Apostles' Creed: Second Article

Take-Home Point
Jesus is alive! Go and tell.

1 Opening (15 minutes)

Welcome Time

What you do: Before class, set up two activity areas. In one, put out copies of Activity Page 7 and crayons. Make copies of Activity Page Fun (below and on CD) for parents or classroom helpers. Adjust talk as necessary.

In the other area, set out a tub of rice on a big towel with plastic Easter eggs.

Play the CD from your Teacher Tools. As the children arrive, greet each one. Give them a sticker to put on the attendance chart.

Say Hi, [Rosalina]. I'm glad to see you! I wonder . . . what happened long ago on Easter? Today you'll hear a Bible story about that.

Direct children to the tables where you have the activities. Encourage parents or caregivers to stay and do the welcome activity with their child.

Activity Page Fun Get a copy of Activity Page 7, and show it to your child. Talk about what opposites are and give examples. Then, tell your child to match the opposites on the page.

Say Point to the tree. Let your child do so. **Now, look at the pictures on the bottom of the page. Which one is the opposite of the tree with leaves? Let's cut it off and glue it next to this tree.** Help your child do so. Continue to describe each picture, and have your child find its opposite. He or she may draw lines to match the opposites, if you wish.

Today, you will hear about some more opposites. Listen closely, and you can tell me what you learned when Sunday School is over.

© 2017 Concordia Publishing House. Reproduced by permission. Available on the Teacher CD.

MATERIALS NEEDED

1 Opening	2 God Speaks	3 We Live	4 Closing
Teacher Tools Attendance chart CD	**Teacher Tools** Storytelling figures 7-1 to 7-8 Background B CD	**Teacher Tools** CD	**Teacher Tools** CD
Student Pack Attendance sticker	**Student Pack** Lesson Leaflet 7 Stickers	**Student Pack** Craft Page 7	**Student Pack** Take-home items
Other Supplies Activity Page 7 (TG) Tub of rice Plastic Easter eggs Resource Page 1 (TG)	**Other Supplies** Activity Page 7 (TG) Scarves *The Easter Surprise* Arch book (optional)	**Other Supplies** Paper plate with happy/sad faces Cups (optional) Hole punch & yarn Paper Plus supplies (optional) Jelly beans	

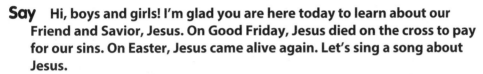

Active Learning Show children how to open the eggs to scoop and pour the rice. Talk about how the eggs are full and empty.

Say On the day we call Good Friday, Jesus died and was put inside a tomb. In today's Bible story, some friends go to Jesus' tomb, but Jesus is not there. The tomb is empty!

Use your classroom signal to let the children know it's time to clean up and gather in your story area. Sing a cleanup song (Resource Page 1).

Gathering in God's Name

What you do: Begin with this opening. To teach about the Church Year, use the materials in the Church Year Worship Kit (see the introduction).

Say Hi, boys and girls! I'm glad you are here today to learn about our Friend and Savior, Jesus. On Good Friday, Jesus died on the cross to pay for our sins. On Easter, Jesus came alive again. Let's sing a song about Jesus.

Sing "Jesus in Jerusalem" (*S&W*, p. 38; CD 13) or "Jesus Christ Is Risen Today" (*LSB* 457; CD 3)

Invite the children to say the Invocation and Amen with you. Tell them "Amen" is the special word we say to ask Jesus to hear our prayers just like He promised.

Begin In the name of the Father and of the Son and of the Holy Spirit. Amen.

Offering Have a child bring the offering basket forward. Sing an offering song.

Pray Dear Jesus, thank You for dying on the cross to pay for our sins. We are happy You rose again on Easter and are alive! We are happy we can live with You in heaven. Alleluia! Amen.

Celebrate Birthdays, Baptism birthdays, and special occasions

(2) God Speaks (20 minutes)

Story Clue

What you do: You will need Activity Page 7. Show it to the children.

Say This page shows pictures of opposites. Review some of them. Let's see what other opposites you know. I will do an action, and you do the opposite. Lead the children in the following actions:
> *Stand—sit.*
> *Flap arms slowly—flap arms quickly.*
> *Reach up—bend down.*
> **Good job, everyone!** Have everyone sit down.

Ask Do you remember what happened on the day we call Good Friday? Jesus suffered and died on the cross for us, didn't He? Today, we will hear how Jesus did the opposite. On Easter, Jesus came alive again!

Bible Story Time

What you do: You will need Background B and storytelling figures 7-1 to 7-8 from your Teacher Tools. Open your Bible to Matthew 28:1–10. Involve the children during the storytelling by having them do the actions with you and adding the figures to the background. Use a restickable glue stick (see introduction), double-sided tape, or loops of tape to attach the figures. *Option:* Tell the story using the Arch Book *The Easter Surprise* (CPH, 59-2275).

Say **On the day we call Good Friday, Jesus died on the cross. His friends took Jesus off the cross and put Him in a tomb—a little cave in a hillside. Then they rolled a big stone in front of the opening.** Put stone (7-1) on background. **Some soldiers came to guard the opening so no one could take Jesus' body.** March in place; then, stand like a soldier. Add soldiers (7-2 and 7-3).

Very early on Sunday morning, when the sun was just starting to shine (circle arms over head)**, something wonderful happened. Suddenly, the ground began to rumble and shake.** Shake and sway from side to side. **There was a very bright light. Then one of God's angels came from heaven. He rolled away the big stone from the door of the tomb and sat on it!** Move stone to side; place angel (7-4) on stone. **The soldiers were so afraid that they fainted and fell to the ground.** Lay soldiers down. **Later, they got up and ran away.** Remove soldiers and angel.

That same morning, Mary and some other women were walking to the tomb. Walk in place. **They felt sad because they missed Jesus. They were going to His tomb to put spices on the cloths He was wrapped up in. As the women walked along, they wondered how they could move the stone in front of Jesus' tomb. But when they got there, they had a big surprise. The stone was already rolled away!** Add figures of women (7-5, 7-6, and 7-7). **Mary was so surprised that she started to run back to tell Jesus' disciples.** Have 7-5 "run off." **The other women peeked into the tomb and saw two angels.**

One angel said, "Do not be afraid! Add angel (7-4) near tomb. **I know you are looking for Jesus. He is not here, for He has risen!"** Lead children in repeating the Bible Words.

How surprised the women were! Look surprised. **Jesus was alive! The angel said, "Come see where He was lying." Then the angel told them, "Go and tell His friends what has happened."**

The women were so happy. They started to run back to tell the disciples the happy news too. Remove women. Step in place. **Suddenly, they heard a voice say, "Greetings!"** Add Jesus (7-8). **It was Jesus! The women ran to Jesus. Then they knelt down and worshiped Him.** Add kneeling women (7-6 and 7-7) in front of Jesus.

Jesus told them, "Don't be afraid! Go and tell My friends the disciples that I am alive." Now the women were not sad anymore. They were happy! Smile. **They ran to find the disciples.** Remove women. **Then they told them the happy news: "Jesus is alive!"** Repeat, "Jesus is alive!"

This is happy news for us too! Jesus suffered and died on the cross for us. Then He came alive again. Our sins are forgiven! Now, we can live with Jesus in heaven forever!

Key Point

The resurrection reveals that the Father has accepted the Son's sacrifice for our sins, and it fills us with confident hope that, as Christ has been raised from the dead, we, too, will rise to eternal life.

Growing in CHRIST

Bible Story Review

What you do: You will need Lesson Leaflet 7, stickers, and crayons. Begin by showing the picture on the leaflet. Ask these questions to review.

Ask **What happened early on Easter morning?** The ground rumbled and shook; an angel came from heaven and rolled away the stone to Jesus' tomb; some women came to Jesus' tomb.

What did the angel tell the women? "Jesus is not here, for He has risen."

What happy event happened next? Jesus appeared to the women.

What did Jesus tell the women to do? Go and tell His disciples that He was alive.

Then hand out the leaflets and crayons. Point to the circles in the sidebar. Give children stickers to match. Have them put their fingers on the top circle.

Say **The word says** *blue*. **Find something blue in the picture.**

Children can draw lines to match the blue circle to what they found in the art. Do the same with the green, purple, and red circles.

Option: For a movement activity, have the children act out the earth shaking as you review the story.

Active Learning Ide

Say **When Jesus died, the sky got very dark. The ground began to shake. Pretend you are the ground, shaking and rumbling.** Lead the children in stamping their feet and rumbling like an earthquake; then, have them be quiet again. **When it was quiet again, Jesus' friends came and put Him in a tomb. On Easter morning, the earth began to shake again.** Rumble and shake again. **Then an angel came and rolled away the stone in front of Jesus' tomb. Surprise! Jesus is alive!**

Bible Words

What you do: You will need a Bible, Lesson Leaflet 7, and stickers. Read the Bible Words from Matthew 28:6. Play them on track 4 of the CD.

Say **In our Bible story, we heard the angel say these words** (read)**: "He is not here, for He has risen, as He said." Say the words with me: [The angel said,] "He is not here, for He has risen, as He said."**

Turn to the back of the Lesson Leaflet. Point to each word in the Bible Words activity, and say it. Have the children echo it.

Show the children how to cover the word *He* with a sticker of Jesus. Continue by putting the closed tomb on the word *here*, the second Jesus sticker on *He*, and the last, open tomb sticker on *risen*. Children can color the angel. Read the verse one more time.

Option: Play the Bible Words on the CD (track 4). Give the children colorful scarves to wave as they sing along.

3 We Live (20 minutes)

Help children grow in their understanding of what the Bible story means for their lives. Choose the activities that work best with your class.

Growing through God's Word

What you do: Take a paper plate. Draw a happy face on one side and a sad face on the other side. Cue the CD if you are using it.

Say Show sad face. **On Good Friday, Jesus suffered and died on the cross. This hurt Jesus a lot. It made Jesus' friends sad. It makes us sad too. Jesus died on the cross to take the punishment for all our sins—the bad things we think and say and do.**

Show happy face. **But on Easter, we have happy news. Jesus didn't stay dead. He came alive again! That good news made Jesus' friends happy. It makes us happy too! We are thankful and full of joy that Jesus showed His power over sin and death and the devil by becoming alive again.**

At Easter, we have a big word that we say in church when we are happy about something. This word is *Alleluia.* **Let's stand and say, "Alleluia!" because God forgives our sins. Can you say it again quietly? Now, let's say it as loud as we can. We are happy that Jesus loves us so much that He came to be our Savior. We are happy that someday we will live with Him in heaven.**

Jesus told the women to go and tell His friends the happy news that He was alive. We can tell others this happy news too. Let's sing a song about that.

Sing "I Can Tell" (*LOSP*, p. 99) or "Do You Know Who Died for Me?" (*LOSP*, p. 93; CD 8)

Craft Time

What you do: Give children Craft Page 7 and crayons or markers. To make the project into a mobile, you will also need scissors, a hole punch, construction paper, and yarn. *Option:* Cut the pictures apart ahead of time and let the children glue them to a larger piece of poster paper to make an Easter picture instead of a mobile. Or glue the pictures to upside-down paper cups to make sets of storytelling puppets.

Have the children point to the words as you read them. Then, tell them to trace the letters in the words with a marker. Help them identify each scene from today's Bible story and color the pictures before cutting them apart. Have the children color the children to look like themselves in church on Easter morning.

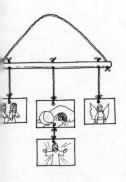

Provide help to cut apart and assemble the pieces into a mobile. Reinforce the crossbar strip by gluing it to construction paper and trimming to size. Punch holes where indicated, and tie yarn through the holes. Tie the open tomb to the middle hole of the crossbar. Use a longer piece of yarn to tie the Jesus picture below it. Then tie the angel on one side and the Mary/children figure on the other side. Tie the ends of a piece of yarn through both sides of the crossbar piece for a hanger.

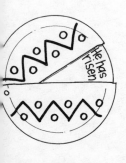

Paper Plus option: Make a "He Has Risen" Easter egg. You will need markers, stickers, a paper fastener, and two paper plates for each project. Write "He has risen" on one plate. This will be the inside of the egg. The other plate will be the shell of the egg. Have the children decorate this plate to look like an Easter egg by adding stickers and coloring Easter egg designs on it.

Growing in CHRIST.

Cut the decorated plate in half. Slightly overlap the two halves of the cut apart plate, and fasten them to the bottom plate using a paper fastener. See illustration. The fastener serves as a hinge so the decorated plate will open like a clamshell to reveal the inside message. (From *Praise God with a Paper Plate*, by Anita Reith Stohs, p. 56. © 1992 CPH.)

Snack Time

What you do: Serve jelly beans. Use the colors to teach about God's plan of salvation: dark or multicolored beans remind us of our sin; red, that Jesus died for us; white, that Jesus rose for us on Easter; and yellow, that Jesus gives us a home in heaven.

Live It Out

What you do: Have children use the craft they made today to tell the Bible story to a friend or relative, or video-record the children singing "Love in a Box" (*LOSP*, p. 35; CD 15). Email the video clip to parents this week along with a note about what you are learning in class about Jesus, our Savior and Friend.

4 Closing (5 minutes)

Going Home

What you do: Send take-home pages and crafts home with the children. Use your CD player and CD to play the song.

Say   Today we learned what happened on the first Easter Day. Jesus came alive again. He told the women, "Go and tell." Let's say, "Jesus is alive. Go and tell" together. Do so.

Sing   "Love in a Box" (*LOSP*, p. 35; CD 15)

Pray   Pray this responsive prayer with the children.
Teacher: Long ago on Easter Day,
Children: Jesus rose for me.
Teacher: An angel told the good news:
Children: Jesus rose for me.
Teacher: All according to God's plan,
Children: Jesus rose for me.
Teacher: To take away all of my sins,
Children: Jesus rose for me.
All: Amen.

Reflection

Does your teaching meet the needs of children with special needs? What should you do the same? What should you change?

Lesson 8

Preparing the Lesson

The Empty Tomb

John 20:1–18

Date of Use

Key Point

On the first Easter, Jesus revealed to Mary Magdalene and to His disciples that He was alive. Through the Word, the Spirit gives us faith to believe in Christ's resurrection and comforts us when we mourn the death of loved ones.

Law/Gospel

Death is a consequence of sin and causes me sorrow. **God comforts me with the promise of the resurrection to eternal life for all who believe in Christ.**

Context

Today's account centers on the empty tomb on Easter morning and Jesus' announcement of His resurrection. After Mary Magdalene encounters the open tomb, she goes to Simon Peter and John and declares, "They have taken the Lord out of the tomb" (John 20:2).

Immediately, Simon Peter and John run to the tomb. John reaches the tomb first, but only looks in. Then Simon Peter arrives and goes into the tomb. Peter sees the linen cloths and face cloth, folded up. When John then went into the tomb and saw the signs of Jesus' resurrection, he "saw and believed" (v. 8).

Commentary

What grief there must have been for Jesus' disciples on that first Easter morning. On Friday, they had witnessed the crucifixion of their Lord and Master, and now His grave had been opened, and His body was gone. Disbelief was characteristic of all the disciples on Easter. When Mary told them that the body of Jesus was not in the tomb, the most natural conclusion to Mary's claim (v. 2) was that someone had come and stolen Jesus' body. But the folded-up head cloth indicates that grave robbers had not taken the body of Jesus, but that He was alive.

And so, John, who is the author of the Gospel account, says that he entered the tomb after Peter, saw the burial linens, especially the neatly folded head cloth, "and believed" (v. 8). And to drive home his point that the Easter story sparks and enlivens faith, John says, "For as yet they did not understand the Scripture, that He must rise from the dead" (v. 9). Yes, they had heard Jesus predict His Passion, crucifixion, and resurrection—multiple times—but somehow what Jesus really meant did not quite click in their minds at that point. Now, though, they did understand, and they believed.

Today, Jesus comes to us in His Word and Sacraments. Through the Word, the Spirit gives us faith to believe in the resurrection of Christ and comforts us when we mourn the death of loved ones. Your students may fear death, or they may be mourning the loss of a relative or friend. The disciples' grief and sorrow and Jesus' announcement of life instead of death provide an opportunity for you to discuss death and the hope we have in Christ.

Of great significance are the words Jesus speaks to Mary Magdalene in the garden after the disciples had returned to their homes. He calls the disciples "My brothers" and refers to God as "My Father and your Father" and "My God and your God" (v. 17). Because Christ shares in our humanity, He is our Brother (Hebrews 2:10–18) and has reconciled us to God.

God is our Father, and we receive countless blessings as His children, including the promised inheritance of heaven. Our sure hope, then, is this: because of the sacrificial death and resurrection of Jesus, we will join with Mary and all the saints in saying, "I have seen the Lord" (John 20:18).

To hear an in-depth discussion of this Bible account, visit cph.org/podcast and listen to our Seeds of Faith podcast each week.

Lesson 8

The Empty Tomb

John 20:1–18

Connections

Bible Words
Christ has been raised from the dead.
1 Corinthians 15:20 (CD 6)

Faith Word
Resurrection

Hymn
Jesus Christ Is Risen Today
(*LSB* 457; CD 3)

Catechism
Apostles' Creed:
Second Article

Take-Home Point
Jesus is alive!

1 Opening (15 minutes)

Welcome Time

What you do: Before class, set up two activity areas. In one, put out copies of Activity Page 8A and crayons. Make copies of Activity Page Fun (below and on CD) for parents or classroom helpers. Adjust talk as necessary.

In the other area, hide plastic eggs for the children to find. Fill the eggs with a variety of small items, but leave some empty. Set out baskets children can use to collect eggs.

Play the CD from your Teacher Tools. As the children arrive, greet each one. Give them a sticker to put on the attendance chart.

Say Hi, [Nolan]. I'm glad to see you! I wonder . . . do you know what happened long ago on Easter? Today you'll hear a Bible story about that.

Direct children to the tables where you have the activities. Encourage parents or caregivers to stay and do the welcome activity with their child.

Activity Page Fun Get a copy of Activity Page 8A, and show it to your child.

Say This picture has a surprise in it. Color each shape that has a dot in it. When you are finished, you will see the surprise. Work with your child to color the picture. **Today you will hear about a surprise some of Jesus' disciples had when they went to His tomb. I wonder . . . what it was.**

MATERIALS NEEDED

1 Opening	2 God Speaks	3 We Live	4 Closing
Teacher Tools Attendance chart CD	**Teacher Tools** Poster C CD	**Student Pack** Craft Page 8 Stickers	**Teacher Tools** CD
Student Pack Attendance sticker	**Student Pack** Lesson Leaflet 8	**Other Supplies** Resource Page 8B (TG) or cross & crucifix (optional) Ribbon (optional) Hole punch Paper Plus supplies (optional) Bread, jelly & cross cookie cutters	**Student Pack** Take-home items
Other Supplies Activity Page 8A (TG) Plastic eggs & items to fill them Baskets Resource Page 1 (TG)	**Other Supplies** Sprout or another puppet Spices (optional) *John's Easter Story* or *Mary Magdalene's Easter Story* (optional)		

Active Learning Before class, hide plastic eggs for the children to find. Fill the eggs with a variety of small items, but leave some empty. Give the children baskets to look for the eggs. When you open the eggs, talk about the surprises you find inside.

Say **In our Bible story today, some of Jesus' friends had a big surprise when they went to Jesus' tomb. The tomb was empty!**

Use your classroom signal to let the children know it's time to clean up and gather in your story area. Sing a cleanup song (Resource Page 1).

Gathering in God's Name

What you do: Begin with this opening. To teach about the Church Year, use the materials in the Church Year Worship Kit (see the introduction).

Say **Hi, boys and girls! I'm glad you are here today to learn about our Friend and Savior, Jesus.**

Sing "Love in a Box" (*LOSP*, p. 35; CD 15) or "Jesus Christ Is Risen Today" (*LSB* 457; CD 3)

Invite the children to say the Invocation and Amen with you. Tell them "Amen" is the special word we say to ask Jesus to hear our prayers just like He promised.

Begin **In the name of the Father and of the Son and of the Holy Spirit. Amen.**

Offering Have a child bring the offering basket forward. Sing an offering song.

Pray **Dear Jesus,* thank You for dying on the cross for us* and for coming alive again on Easter.* Thank You for loving us so much!* We are glad to be in Sunday School* so we can learn more about You!* Amen.*** *Have children echo each phrase.

Celebrate Birthdays, Baptism birthdays, and special occasions

2 God Speaks (20 minutes)

Story Clue

What you do: Use Sprout or another puppet to introduce the Bible story.

Teacher: Look who's here. It's our friend Sprout.

Sprout: Hi, Teacher. Hi, girls and boys.

Teacher: I heard it was your birthday this week. Did you have a happy time?

Sprout: Oh boy, did I ever! My grandma and grandpa came over. And my cousin Lily and her mom. We played games, and then we had a big, delicious dinner. And guess what happened while we were eating!

Teacher: I have no idea, Sprout. Children, can you guess what happened? No one seems to know, Sprout, so please tell us.

Sprout: The doorbell rang. And guess what! My dad opened the door, and there was my aunt Chrysanthemum. What a surprise! She drove one hundred miles to surprise us for my birthday!

Teacher: Wow! That sounds like a very nice surprise! I'm glad you had such a great birthday celebration, Sprout.

Sprout: Thanks, Teacher. I gotta run. My aunt is taking me to the park today before she goes home. *(Children wave and say good-bye to Sprout.)*

Teacher: Hearing about Sprout's surprise visit from Aunt Chrysanthemum reminds me about our Bible story. Someone in the story gets a surprise too!

Bible Story Time

What you do: Practice telling the story using the actions. Have Poster C ready to show. If you wish, bring some spices (e.g., cloves, cinnamon) for the children to smell. *Option:* Tell the story using one of these Arch Books: *John's Easter Story* (CPH, 59-2248) or *Mary Magdalene's Easter Story* (CPH, 59-1592).

Say **It was very early in the morning.** Stretch and yawn. Have children do the actions with you. **Most people were still asleep.** Put head on hands with eyes closed. **But not Mary Magdalene (MAG duh lehn)! She was up** (stand)**, dressed** (pretend to dress)**, and out the door** (walk in place)**. She was in a hurry to get to the tomb in the garden where Jesus was buried.** Walk in place faster; then, have children sit again.

On Friday, her friend Jesus had been nailed to a cross. Make fist and hammer. **That made Mary Magdalene very sad.** Make sad face. **After Jesus died on the cross, His body had been put into a tomb. Then, a big stone was rolled in front of the opening.**

Now, Mary was taking some sweet-smelling spices to put on the clothes that Jesus was wrapped up in. Hold hand like a cup; pretend to sniff. If you brought some spices, let the children smell them. **Hurry, hurry, hurry.** Step in place. **Mary hurried through the streets.** Step in place faster. **She hurried through the garden gate. She hurried all the way to Jesus' tomb.**

Mary wondered who would roll away the big stone in front of the opening. But when she got near the tomb, she had a big surprise. Rub eyes in disbelief. **The big stone was already rolled away from the opening!** Roll hands.

Mary was so surprised that she hurried back to tell Jesus' disciples. Hurry, hurry, hurry. Step in place. **Mary hurried through the garden gate.** Step in place faster. **She hurried through the streets. She hurried to tell Peter and John, "Jesus is gone. He's not in the tomb anymore!"**

Right away, Peter and John hurried to Jesus' tomb to see for themselves! Hurry, hurry, hurry. Step in place. **Peter and John hurried through the streets.** Step in place. **They hurried through the garden gate. They hurried to look inside Jesus' tomb.**

When they looked inside the tomb, Peter and John could hardly believe what they saw. Rub eyes in disbelief. **The tomb was empty! They saw the clothes that Jesus had been wrapped up in. But they did not see Jesus! Then, John knew that Jesus was alive again!** Show Poster C.

The disciples hurried back home. Mary Magdalene stayed in the garden. She was crying. Wipe eyes. **She felt sad because she did not know Jesus was alive. Then, Mary heard a man's voice. He asked her, "Why are you crying?"**

Mary thought it was the man who took care of the garden. "Oh, sir," she

Key Point

On the first Easter, Jesus revealed to Mary Magdalene and to His disciples that He was alive. Through the Word, the Spirit gives us faith to believe in Christ's resurrection and comforts us when we mourn the death of loved ones.

eat Multisensory Learning!

Growing in CHRIST.

said, "if you have put Jesus' body somewhere, please tell me where."

Then the man said, "Mary." Right away, Mary knew it was Jesus! Mary Magdalene stopped crying and started to smile. Point to smile. She was so glad to see her friend Jesus alive!

Then Mary hurried back to tell the disciples. Hurry, hurry, hurry. Step in place. She hurried away from the tomb. She hurried through the garden gate. Step in place faster. She hurried through the streets. When she saw Jesus' disciples, she said, "I have seen Jesus. He is alive!"

Jesus' friends were happy that Jesus was alive. We are happy that Jesus is alive too. Now our sins are forgiven. Now everyone who believes in Jesus will live in heaven with Him.

Bible Story Review

What you do: You will need Poster C, the Lessons Leaflets, and crayons. Show the poster and ask these questions to review.

Ask   **Who are these men?** Peter and John

Where is Jesus? He is risen.

What surprises does Mary Magdalene get on Easter? The stone was rolled away from the tomb. Jesus appeared to her in the garden. He was alive!

What does Mary do after Jesus appears to her in the garden? She hurried to tell the disciples that Jesus is alive.

Whom can you tell about Jesus? Accept answers.

Hand out the leaflets and crayons. Draw children's attention to the pictures in the sidebar. Help them find the pictured items in the artwork, count how many of each they find, and circle the correct numeral. On side 2, have them use their finger, then a crayon, to take Peter and John to the empty tomb.

Option: Sing the song in the Do Together section of the leaflet.

Bible Words

What you do: Read the words from 1 Corinthians 15:20. Use the activity to help the children learn the words, or play them on track 6 of the CD.

Ask   **On Good Friday, Jesus died on the cross to pay for our sins. What happened on Easter Sunday? Jesus came back to life again! Our Bible words tell about this: "Christ has been raised from the dead"** (1 Corinthians 15:20). **Let's say this together.** Repeat the verse.

Have children stand and say the verse with you; then do the action rhyme together. *Option:* Listen to the words on the CD and sing along.

Say   **"Christ has been raised from the dead." Let's say this with our loud voices.** Say the verse. **Now use your whisper voices to say the Bible Words.** Say the verse again. **Very good. Now watch what I do; then do it too.**

When Jesus died, they buried Him	*Crouch down low.*
Inside an empty cave.	*Make motion outlining "cave."*
But Easter came and—happy day—	*Make circle with arms to represent sun.*
My Jesus is ALIVE!	*Again, raise arms above head and jump.*

From *Fingers Tell the Story*, © 1989 CPH, p. 30.

③ We Live (20 minutes)

Help children grow in their understanding of what the Bible story means for their lives. Choose the activities that work best with your class.

What you do: Copy Activity Page 8B, or bring a cross and a crucifix to class.

Show the children the pictures of the crosses on Activity Page 8B, or display a cross and crucifix if you have them. Ask them what is the same and what is different. Explain that the crucifix shows how Jesus suffered and died for our sins on the cross, and that the empty cross reminds us that Jesus didn't stay dead, but He rose again on Easter, as He said He would.

Say **Jesus' coming alive again at Easter is called His resurrection. Because Jesus came to be our Savior, God forgives our sins. Someday, all who believe in Jesus as their Savior will live with Jesus forever in heaven.**

Option: Take a field trip to the sanctuary, pastor's office, or other places where there are crosses. Have the children count how many crosses they find.

ive Learning Idea!

Craft Time

What you do: You will need Craft Page 8, the stickers for this lesson, scissors, and a hole punch. If you wish, use wide ribbon instead of the headband piece to attach the visors. If the children you teach have poor cutting skills, cut out the visors ahead of time.

Hand out the Craft Page. Give the children word stickers to add to the boxes. Match by color and shape. Ask the children to put their finger on each word as you read the message (He has risen), and have the children echo it. Have them color the visor, cut it out, and decorate it with the remaining stickers.

Point out that visors keep the sun out of our eyes so we can see. What did Peter and John see when they ran to the tomb? It was empty! Jesus had risen. How do we see Jesus? God gives us faith through Baptism and His Word to see and believe in Jesus as our Savior.

On the opposite side, have children color the picture. Help them tape the headband pieces to each side of the visor where indicated. You may need to cut the headband piece in half and add an extension piece. Size to fit.

Option: Punch holes at the X's, and tie wide ribbon to the ends of the visor. Leave ribbon long enough to be able to fit visor around child's head and tie in back.

Paper Plus option: Make stone paperweights. You will need crayons and a smooth stone for each child. You will also need a cookie sheet covered with aluminum foil and access to an oven, plus newspapers and old socks that the children can share. They will use the socks to polish their rocks.

Have children use a crayon to rub a design such as a cross or heart or flower on their stones. Put all the stones on the cookie sheet and bake at 200 degrees F. for 15 minutes. Cool the stones on stacks of newspaper. When stones are almost completely cool, give children old socks to put over their hands. Have them polish their stones with the socks to make a smooth design that will shine.

Snack Time

What you do: Show children how to use a cross cookie cutter to cut out a cross from a slice of bread. Spread with jelly for a tasty snack.

Live It Out

What you do: The paschal candle is lit at Baptisms, weddings, funerals, and Easter as a reminder of Christ's presence with us. It is lit on Holy Saturday to symbolize Christ's passing over from the grave back to life, and it remains lit for forty days after Easter to remind us of Christ's presence with His people until His ascension. Ask your pastor or an altar guild member if you can show the paschal candle to the children, or take pictures of it on your tablet device to show them. Talk with the children about the "pictures" (symbols) on the candle. Are there crosses on the candle? How many?

4 Closing (5 minutes)

Going Home

What you do: Send take-home pages and crafts home with the children. Use your CD player and CD to play the song.

Sing "Do You Know Who Died for Me?" (*LOSP*, p. 93; CD 8) or "Love in a Box" (*LOSP*, p. 35; CD 15)

Ask **What was Mary Magdalene's surprise on Easter?** (The stone was rolled away; Jesus was alive.) **Mary Magdalene and Jesus' friends Peter and John were happy to find out that Jesus was alive. That is also good news for you and me. Let's say that together: "Jesus is alive!" Do so. Because Jesus is alive, we will live with Him in heaven one day.**

Pray Have the children echo each phrase:
Dear Jesus,* we are so happy* that You are alive.*
Thank You for loving us.* We love You too.* Amen.*

Reflection

What part of the lesson were the children most receptive to? Why? Look for similar activities for future lessons.

Color only the sections with a dot.

Preparing the Lesson

Jesus Appears on the Emmaus Road

Luke 24:13–35

Date of Use

Key Point

The disciples recognized Jesus through the Scriptures and the breaking of the bread. Christ comes to us and abides with us through Word and Sacrament and continues to open our eyes and strengthen our faith.

Law/**Gospel**

Sin blinds me to the truth and keeps me from recognizing and believing in Jesus as my Savior. **Jesus opens my eyes through God's Word and Sacraments so that I might believe and trust in Him.**

Context

Cleopas and his unnamed companion were making the seven-mile walk from Jerusalem to the small village of Emmaus, west of Jerusalem. It was Easter Sunday, late in the afternoon. After these two disciples realized that they had seen Jesus, they returned to Jerusalem to tell the apostles.

Commentary

Cleopas and his companion were sad and confused as they walked along the road to Emmaus. Even though they had heard the report of the women and some of the apostles (probably Peter and John) that Jesus was alive, they did not believe it. Their words reveal their unbelief: "We *had hoped* that He was the one to redeem Israel" (Luke 24:21, emphasis added).

When Jesus came up to them on the road, they did not recognize Him. However, this was not just a case of mistaken identity: "Their eyes *were kept* from recognizing Him" (v. 16, emphasis added). By divine intervention, these disciples were not permitted to recognize Jesus immediately. Instead, Jesus desired first to instruct these disciples on the necessity of His suffering and death and then to be recognized in the breaking of the bread.

Jesus' discussion with these two disciples shows that He is the center of all Scripture: "And beginning with Moses and all the Prophets, He interpreted to them in all the Scriptures the things concerning Himself" (v. 27). "Moses and all the Prophets" is a reference to the entire Old Testament. In other words, as they walked along the road, Jesus, using the Old Testament Scriptures, led these disciples to see all that the prophets had foretold was fulfilled in Him.

The discussion on the road led to an invitation for Jesus to stay with the disciples. Although He was invited as a guest, when it was time to eat, Jesus became the host. He took the bread, blessed and broke it, and gave it to them. Through the breaking of the bread, these disciples' eyes were opened. They were no longer sad and hopeless but were filled with great joy. They immediately returned to Jerusalem to tell the other disciples.

Unlike the Emmaus disciples, we are not kept from recognizing Jesus by an act of divine intervention. However, we are blinded because of sin. We cannot see and believe the truth unless Christ takes away our spiritual blindness. The way in which He accomplishes this is the same as it was for the Emmaus disciples—through the Word. The Old and New Testaments both have as their focus Jesus Christ and His suffering, death, and resurrection for our salvation. As Jesus opens the Scriptures for us, our hearts burn within us with a living faith that believes and trusts in Him.

These disciples recognized Jesus through the Scriptures and the breaking of the bread. This foreshadows what would become the two focal points of Christian worship—hearing the Word and receiving the Lord's Supper. Through these means, Christ comes to us and abides with us. Through Word and Sacrament, He continues to open our eyes and strengthen us in the one true faith.

To hear an in-depth discussion of this Bible account, visit cph.org/podcast and listen to our Seeds of Faith podcast each week.

Lesson 9

Jesus Appears on the Emmaus Road

Luke 24:13–35

Connections

Bible Words
God gave us eternal life
. . . in His Son. 1 John 5:11
(CD 7)

Faith Word
Believe

Hymn
Jesus Christ Is Risen Today
(*LSB* 457; CD 3)

Catechism
Apostles' Creed:
Second Article

Take-Home Point
God's Word shows me
that Jesus is the Savior.

 **1 Opening** (15 minutes)

Welcome Time

What you do: Before class, set up two activity areas. In one, put out copies of Activity Page 9A, stickers, and crayons. Make copies of Activity Page Fun (below and on CD) for parents or classroom helpers. Adjust talk as necessary.

In the other area, set out a variety of Bibles (large print, braille, family Bibles, children's picture Bibles, and the like). For the optional activity, find a picture of Jesus in a book or online, and cut it into eight puzzle pieces.

Play the CD from your Teacher Tools. As the children arrive, bend down and greet each one to let them know you are glad they have come. Give them a sticker to put on the attendance chart. Show them where to put their offering.

Say Hi, [Maeva]. I'm glad to see you! I wonder . . . do you have a favorite Bible story? Today you'll hear how the Bible helps us learn about Jesus.

Direct children to the tables where you have the activities. Encourage parents or caregivers to stay and do the welcome activity with their child.

Activity Page Fun Get a copy of the Activity Page and a Jesus sticker. Have your child name each item. Talk about the items that help us see.

Ask Which items help us see? Let child tell, giving help as needed. Have your child color the things that help us see.

Say In our story today, you will find out how the Bible helps us to see in a special way. It shows us that Jesus is our Savior. Give child a sticker of Jesus to add by the Bible.

MATERIALS NEEDED

1 Opening	2 God Speaks	3 We Live	4 Closing
Teacher Tools Attendance chart CD	**Teacher Tools** Storytelling Figures 9-1 to 9-5 Background A CD	**Teacher Tools** CD	**Teacher Tools** CD
Student Pack Attendance sticker Jesus sticker	**Student Pack** Lesson Leaflet 9	**Student Pack** Craft Page 9 Stickers	**Student Pack** Take-home items Scarves or crepe-paper streamers
Other Supplies Activity Page 9A (TG) Bibles Picture of Jesus Resource Page 1 (TG)	**Other Supplies** Activity Page 9B (TG) Sprout or another puppet *The Easter Stranger* Arch Book (optional) Newspapers (optional)	**Other Supplies** Picture of Jesus Puzzle pieces of Jesus' face Activity Page 9B Paper Plus supplies (optional) Cloverleaf rolls & honey	

Active Learning Set out a variety of Bibles (large print, braille, family Bibles, soft cover, children's picture Bible or Bible story book, and the like).

Ask Do all these Bible books look alike? No. They all look different, but they all tell us about Jesus and how He came to be our Savior.

Option: Hide the puzzle pieces you have made from a Jesus picture around the room. Tuck some pieces inside Bibles or Bible story books with part of the piece still visible. Have the children walk in pairs to find the pieces.

Say Walk with a friend around the room and look for the pieces of a puzzle that I hid. In our Bible story today, two men are walking and trying to figure out a puzzle too.

As the children put the pieces together, ask them what they think the picture might be. Point out how it's hard to tell what the picture is until all the pieces are together. When it's done, continue.

Great Idea!

Say Surprise! Who do you see? Yes, Jesus! In our Bible story today, the men are surprised in a special way too.

Use your classroom signal to let the children know it's time to clean up and gather in your story area. Sing a cleanup song (Resource Page 1).

Gathering in God's Name

What you do: Begin with this opening. To teach about the Church Year, use the materials in the Church Year Worship Kit (see the introduction).

15, 3

Say Hi, boys and girls! I'm glad you are here today to learn about our Friend and Savior, Jesus.

Sing "Love in a Box" (*LOSP*, p. 35; CD 15) or "Jesus Christ Is Risen Today" (*LSB* 457; CD 3)

Invite the children to say the Invocation and Amen with you. Tell them "Amen" is the special word we say to ask Jesus to hear our prayers.

Begin In the name of the Father and of the Son and of the Holy Spirit. Amen.

Offering Have a child bring the offering basket forward. Sing an offering song. *Have children echo each phrase in the prayer.

Pray Dear Jesus,* we are glad* to be in Sunday School.* Please help us learn* more about You.* Amen.*

Celebrate Birthdays, Baptism birthdays, and special occasions

② **God Speaks** (20 minutes)

Story Clue

What you do: Copy Activity Page 9B. Color every other stripe red. Color the remaining stripes yellow. Accordion-fold the paper on the dotted lines to make a fan. Turn the fan at an angle so the red shows. Turn it the opposite way so the yellow shows. Talk about the surprise of seeing a different color.

Say In our Bible story today, two men had a surprise too. At first, they could not see Jesus; then later, they could see Him. Let's find out how!

Bible Story Time

What you do: Use Background A and Storytelling Figures 9-1 to 9-5. Use a restickable glue stick (see introduction), double-sided tape, or loops of tape to attach the figures. Put the figures in your Bible or have it beside you to show the children. Tell them this is a true story from God's Word. Do the actions as you tell the story to help keep the children's attention. *Option:* Tell the story using the Arch Book *The Easter Stranger* (CPH, 59-2221).

Say   **On Easter Sunday afternoon, two men were walking along a road.** Add men (9-1 and 9-2) to Background A. **They were going to a town called Emmaus (uh MEY us).** *Crunch, crunch* **went their sandals on the road.** Step in place. **The men were talking about their friend Jesus. They wondered about the things that had happened to Jesus. They felt sad that He had died.**

While the men were walking (step in place) **and talking** (move hand open and shut to imitate talking), **Jesus came and walked next to them.** Add Jesus (9-3). **But the men did not know that it was Jesus.**

"Hello," Jesus said. " What are you talking about?" The men stopped walking and looked sad. Look down and shake head slowly.

Then one of the men said, "Haven't you heard the news? Our friend Jesus did so many wonderful things. He helped many people. He healed those who were sick. But then some men told lies about Him, and He was killed on a cross. We thought He was the Savior God promised to send, but He has been dead for three days now. Hold up three fingers.

"Then, this morning some women we know went to Jesus' tomb, but His body was gone! The women said an angel told them that Jesus is alive!" Point to Jesus figure. **"But how can that be true?" The men did not know that they were talking to Jesus.**

Jesus asked, "Don't you know that this was all part of God's plan?" Then Jesus started to explain God's Word to them. He told them that the Savior had to die and come alive again to save people from their sins. Then He taught them many more things from God's Word.

Soon, the two men came to the place where they were staying. They invited Jesus to stay with them. "It's getting dark," they said. "Please come in and stay with us." Remove all figures.

At suppertime, they all sat down to eat. Add scene of Jesus and men in house (9-4). **Then Jesus let the men see who He was. He took some bread, blessed it, and broke it into pieces. Right away, the men knew it was Jesus!** Point to Jesus on the storytelling figure. **He really was alive! How surprised and happy they were! Then Jesus disappeared again.** Cover Jesus figure on 9-4 with a piece of paper.

The men said to each other, "We should have known that this man was Jesus. He told us so much from the Bible." Remove 9-4. Place disciples (9-1 and 9-2) on board again. **Even though it was already dark, the men hurried back to Jerusalem to tell Jesus' disciples.** Run in place. **They wanted their friends to know that Jesus was alive too.**

When they got there, they rushed inside and told everyone, "We saw Jesus! He really is alive! Add group of disciples (9-5). **He walked on the road with us and explained God's Word to us. But we didn't know who**

Key Point

The disciples recognized Jesus through the Scriptures and the breaking of the bread. Christ comes to us and abides with us through Word and Sacrament and continues to open our eyes and strengthen our faith.

Growing in CHRIST

He was until He broke the bread and gave it to us." When Jesus' disciples heard this news, they were happy too. They were happy that Jesus was alive!

Bible Story Review

What you do: You will need Lesson Leaflet 9 and crayons. Show children the picture on Lesson Leaflet 9. Ask these questions to review.

Ask **What happens while the men are walking to Emmaus?** Jesus started walking with them.

What does Jesus tell them? He explained how God said in His Word that He was going to send a Savior who would pay for our sins.

When do the men know it is Jesus? They recognized Jesus when He held the bread and blessed it.

Hand out the leaflets and crayons. Point to the pictures in the box (man, sandal, and satchel). Help the children find the matching items in the Bible art and count and circle the correct numeral. On side 2, have children use their finger, then their crayon, to trace the men's path through the maze from the house to Jerusalem. Talk about people the children can tell about Jesus.

Option: Use newspapers to build a road from Jerusalem to Emmaus. Have pairs take turns walking on the road, then having Jesus join them. Briefly retell the story as they act out the story actions.

Active Learning Id

Bible Words

What you do: Read 1 John 5:11, "God gave us eternal life . . . in His Son," from your Bible. Play the words on track 7 of the CD, or use the action rhyme to help the children learn the words.

Say **God sent Jesus to be the Savior for all people. Jesus took the punishment for everyone's sin on the cross. The Bible says, "God gave us eternal life . . . in His Son." That means that all who believe in Jesus will live with Him forever.** Say the Bible Words together or listen to them on the CD.

Option: Ask the children to do the actions and say the Bible Words with you.

Say **God**   *Point up.*
    gave us   *Hold hands out.*
    eternal life . . .   *Make a big circle with arms.*
    in His Son.   *Make cross with fingers.*

③ **We Live** (20 minutes)

Help children grow in their understanding of what the Bible story means for their lives. Choose the activities that work best with your class.

Growing through God's Word

What you do: You will need a Bible, some puzzle pieces from the Welcome Time activity, and a picture of Jesus. First, show the puzzle pieces. (If you did not do the puzzle activity during Welcome Time, omit the first paragraph.)

Say Before we put the pieces of our puzzle together this morning, we couldn't tell what the picture would be. But once all the pieces were together, whom did we see? Show the picture of Jesus. **Yes, Jesus!**

In our Bible story today, the two men walking to Emmaus knew lots of things about Jesus. But they did not understand how all these things fit together. After Jesus came and helped them understand, whom did they see? Hold up picture of Jesus **Yes, Jesus!**

Do you remember how Jesus helped the men understand that He was the Savior God promised? Hold up Bible. **Yes, Jesus taught them from God's Word. He helped them to see that it was part of God's plan for the Savior to suffer and die for the sins of all people and then come alive again. Jesus taught them many things from God's Word.** Hold up Bible again.

We learn about Jesus in God's Word too. The Bible tells us that Jesus was true God, but He left His home in heaven to be our Savior. Jesus was born as a little baby. He grew up and taught many about God's love. Then Jesus suffered and died on the cross to pay for our sins and came alive again on Easter. Jesus did all this for us so our sins would be forgiven. Because we believe in Jesus, someday we can live with Him in heaven.

Craft Time

What you do: You will need Craft Page 9, stickers, and crayons. Before class, accordion-fold the Craft Page on the dotted lines to make a fan. To accordion-fold the page, alternate between mountain folds and valley folds, so the page looks like the bellows of an accordion when done. Smooth out the page before giving it to the children. First, show the red and yellow accordion-folded paper used earlier.

Ask Do you remember the fan we used earlier? Show fan made from Activity Page 9B. **Now, you will make your own special fan to take home. It says, "God's Word shows me Jesus."**

Hand out the Craft Page with side 1 faceup. Have the children put their finger on the circle. Give each one a sticker of Jesus to put in the space. Have children point to the cross and color it. Give the children the stickers that say "for" and "me." Have them match the color and shape to put stickers in the right places. Have children point and say with you, "Jesus died for me." Help refold the page so the children can see the two different scenes ("Jesus died for me" and the image of a cross).

Turn to the other side, and have the children color the Bible and match stickers to the remaining shapes. Have children point to each shape and say with you, "God's Word shows me Jesus." Again, refold the page and look at the two different views ("God's Word shows me Jesus" and the image of Jesus).

Paper Plus option: Make Bible story books from old leaflets. Give the children a piece of 11 × 17-inch poster paper and a variety of decorating materials (Easter stickers, markers, stamps, colored tissue paper, and glue). Let the children decorate their "covers." Fold the paper in half and write "My Bible Story Book" on the front.

Put today's leaflet in the booklet. Punch two holes along the side through all thicknesses, and put 1-inch rings through the holes to make a booklet. Tell the children they can put their leaflets in their book each week and make a Bible story book that tells about Jesus.

Snack Time

What you do: Serve cloverleaf rolls with honey. Jesus showed the men who He was when He broke the bread and gave it to them. Remind them that Jesus is a guest at our table when we eat. Lead them in the prayer: "Come, Lord Jesus, be our guest, and let these gifts to us be blessed." Enjoy the snack.

Live It Out

What you do: Encourage children to look for Bibles at home and count how many they have. Have them ask their parents to tell them about their family Bible, and read this week's Bible story from it.

 **4 Closing** (5 minutes)

Going Home

What you do: Send take-home pages and crafts home with the children. Use your CD player and CD to play the hymn. Have scarves or streamers to wave.

Sing "Do You Know Who Died for Me?" (*LOSP*, p. 93; CD 8) or "Jesus Loves Me" (*LOSP*, p. 42; CD 14). As you play the song on the CD, have the children walk in a circle and wave scarves or crepe-paper streamers.

Say **Today, we heard that it was God's plan to send His Son, Jesus, to be our Savior. We learn about that in God's Word. Let's say, "God's Word shows me that Jesus is the Savior" together.** Say take-home point. **Jesus suffered and died on the cross and rose again for us. Because Jesus is alive, everyone who believes in Him will live with Him in heaven one day.**

Pray **Dear Jesus, we're so happy You are alive! Thank You for the Bible, where You show us that You are our Savior. Amen.**

Reflection

How are the children getting along? Are they showing God's love to one another? Continue to help them verbalize "I'm sorry" and "I forgive you."

Color the things that help us see. How does the Bible help us see?

Color dark strips red; color the remaining strips yellow.

Preparing the Lesson

Jesus Appears to Thomas

John 20:19–31

Date of Use

Key Point

We, like Thomas, doubt what we cannot see. Through His Spirit, God gives us eyes of faith that we might see Jesus in Word and Sacrament and believe in Him.

Law/**Gospel**

I sin when I rely on human reason instead of God's Word and what it says about my Savior. **The Holy Spirit gives me eyes of faith to believe that Jesus died and rose for my salvation and fills my heart with peace.**

Context

Following His resurrection, Jesus is no longer confined to the physical limitations of His earthly body. In this account, John reports two miraculous appearances of the risen Christ to His followers.

Commentary

Jesus appeared to the disciples "on the evening of that day" (v. 19), the first Easter evening (see 20:1).

Suddenly, Jesus "came and stood" in the midst of the disciples, even though they were behind locked doors. The language is even clearer that His appearance among the disciples eight days later was in spite of the locked doors. This indicates Jesus' body was (and is) no longer exactly the same as it was prior to His resurrection; it is not bound by the same physical limitations as before.

On appearing, Jesus first said, "Peace be with you" (vv. 19, 26). In a few moments, He would say this again. After Jesus said this, He showed the disciples the wounds on His hands and side that He received during His crucifixion. Both Jesus' appearance and His words gave peace to the disciples.

Jesus then sent the disciples as He had done earlier in His ministry (John 17:18; Matthew 10:5). But this sending is different. From now on, it would be to all people, including the Gentiles.

Next, Jesus gave spiritual authority to the disciples and therefore to His Church on earth. It is important to note that Luther used verses 22–23 in his Small Catechism as the chief Bible passage for the institution of the Office of the Keys.

Thomas, one of the twelve disciples, was not present on that first Easter evening. Though the other disciples told him everything that had happened, Thomas didn't believe on the basis of their words alone. He wanted to see and touch Jesus' wounds.

One week later, Jesus again appeared to the disciples, this time with Thomas present. Though the testimony of the other disciples hadn't convinced Thomas that Jesus had risen, when Thomas saw and touched the Lord's wounds, he did believe and confessed Jesus to be his Lord and God.

Jesus pointed out that Thomas believed because he had seen. Jesus declares those people "blessed" who believe that He is the resurrected Lord, even if they haven't seen. They believe on the basis of words alone.

John concludes this section by pointing out that his Gospel account was written so that many people might come to "believe that Jesus is the Christ, the Son of God" and thus have eternal life.

To hear an in-depth discussion of this Bible account, visit cph.org/podcast and listen to our Seeds of Faith podcast each week.

Lesson 10
Jesus Appears to Thomas
John 20:19–31

Connections

Bible Words
Blessed are those who have not seen and yet have believed.
John 20:29

Faith Word
Peace

Hymn
Jesus Christ Is Risen Today
(*LSB* 457; CD 3)

Catechism
Apostles' Creed:
Second Article

Liturgy
Peace of the Lord

Take-Home Point
God gives me His peace through Jesus.

 1 Opening (15 minutes)

What you do: Before class, set up two activity areas. In one, put out copies of Activity Page 10 and crayons. Make copies of Activity Page Fun (below and on CD) for parents or classroom helpers. Adjust talk as necessary.

In the other area, set out play dough and cross and angel cookie cutters.

Play the CD from your Teacher Tools. As the children arrive, bend down and greet each one at eye level with a smile. Give them a sticker to put on the attendance chart. Show them where to put their offering.

Say Hi, [Carlos]. I'm glad to see you! I wonder . . . how do you know something is true or real?

Direct children to the tables where you have the activities. Encourage parents or caregivers to stay and do the welcome activity with their child.

Activity Page Fun Get a copy of the Activity Page. Show it to your child.

Ask Which man is Jesus? How do you know? What is on Jesus' hands? Let child tell. **Jesus has nail marks on His hands from when He died on the cross to pay for our sins. But Jesus came back to life, didn't He? I wonder who the other man is. What do you think he is doing?** Color the picture together.

You'll hear more about Jesus and this man in today's Bible story, so listen carefully. Then you can tell me about it later.

MATERIALS NEEDED

1 Opening	2 God Speaks	3 We Live	4 Closing
Teacher Tools Attendance chart CD **Student Pack** Attendance sticker **Other Supplies** Activity Page 10 (TG) Play dough Cross & angel cookie cutters Resource Page 1 (TG)	**Student Pack** Lesson Leaflet 10 **Other Supplies** Sprout or another puppet *The Story of the Empty Tomb* Arch Book (optional)	**Student Pack** Craft Page 10 Stickers **Other Supplies** Sprout or another puppet Decorating supplies Paper Plus supplies (optional) O-shaped pretzels or cereal	**Teacher Tools** CD **Student Pack** Take-home materials

Active Learning Show the children how to cut angels and crosses out of play dough with the cookie cutters, and demonstrate making a big stone out of the play dough. Talk about the events of Good Friday and Easter.

Say **You are using your hands to make crosses and angels out of play dough. In our story today, Jesus shows Thomas something special about His hands so Thomas will believe that Jesus is really alive.**

Use your classroom signal for cleanup time. Sing a cleanup song (Resource Page 1). Gather the children for your opening and story time with this song. Sing it to the tune of "Are You Sleeping?" Repeat with each child's name.

Sing **Where is [Madelyn]? Where is [Micah]?**
Look around questioningly each time.
Here they are. Here they are.
Point to children and beckon them to come over.
Why are they so happy? Why are they so happy?
Trace smile on face.
Jesus lives! Jesus lives!

Gathering in God's Name

15, 3

What you do: Begin with this opening. To teach about the Church Year, use the materials in the Church Year Worship Kit (see the introduction).

Say **Hi, boys and girls! I'm glad you are here today! Let's sing.**

Sing "Love in a Box" (*LOSP*, p. 35; CD 15) or "Jesus Christ Is Risen Today" (*LSB* 457; CD 3)

Invite the children to say the Invocation and Amen with you. Tell them "Amen" is the special word we say to ask Jesus to hear our prayers just like He promised.

Begin **In the name of the Father and of the Son and of the Holy Spirit. Amen.**

Offering Have a child bring the offering basket forward. Sing an offering song. Pause at asterisk and have children echo each phrase in the prayer. Tell children you will say a phrase and then they can pray it back to God.

Pray **Dear Jesus,* thank You* for dying for us* and coming alive again on Easter.* Thank You* for loving us so much!* We believe You are our Savior.* Amen.***

Celebrate Birthdays, Baptism birthdays, and special occasions

2 God Speaks (20 minutes)

Story Clue

What you do: Use Sprout today to introduce the story.

Sprout: *(Bouncing excitedly)* Hi, everybody! Guess where I'm going today!

Teacher: Hi, Sprout. You sure seem excited. Let's see . . . are you going to a movie? *(Sprout shakes his head no.)* Are you going to the mall with your mom to buy a special toy? *(Sprout shakes his head no again.)* I can't think of anywhere else, Sprout. Boys and girls, can you guess where Sprout is going?

Sprout: *(Interrupting)* Nope, you are all wrong! You'll never guess where I'm going! It's someplace I've never been before! I'm going to the circus!

Teacher: Oh, Sprout, that sounds like fun!

Sprout: Yeah, that's what my cousin Lily said. She went there last week, and she told me all about it. But I don't believe her. I think she's making it all up! That's why I want to go see for myself.

Teacher: Why don't you believe Lily, Sprout? What did she tell you?

Sprout: Oh, all sorts of crazy things. She said there were lions and tigers jumping through hoops of fire! Then she saw people walking on skinny little ropes high off the ground. And other people were flying and tumbling through the air off of swings! Ha! I don't believe her one bit. I think she's just making it all up! That Lily has a good 'magination!

Teacher: Oh, Sprout, Lily may have a good imagination, but she's telling you the truth. You *will* see wonderful things like that at the circus.

Sprout: Well, I still have to see it with my own eyes before I'll believe all the things she told me!

Teacher: *(Chuckling)* Sprout, you remind me of Thomas. I think you are in for a big surprise today when you go to the circus.

Sprout: Who's Thomas? What surprise did he get?

Teacher: Thomas was one of Jesus' special friends, the disciples. Thomas didn't believe his friends when they told him that Jesus was alive again. But Thomas got a big surprise. Why don't you stay and listen to the Bible story to see what happened? *(Set Sprout where he can "listen.")*

Bible Story Time

What you do: Tell the story in a dramatic way. *Option:* Use the Arch Book *The Story of the Empty Tomb* (CPH, 59-1517) to tell the story.

Say **It was Easter Sunday evening. Jesus' friends, the disciples, were scared. Jesus had died on the cross on Good Friday. Some of the women told them, "Jesus is alive!" but Jesus' disciples had not seen Him. They wondered about what the women told them. And they worried that the soldiers would come after them and hurt them too. So they all gathered in one room, except for Thomas. They had the doors and windows locked so no one could get in.** Pretend to lock door.

All at once, Jesus was with them! Look surprised. **At first, Jesus' friends were afraid.** Step back in fear. **They thought they were seeing a ghost. Then Jesus said, "Peace be with you," and He showed them the nail marks in His hands and feet.** Hold out hands, palms up. **He showed them the mark in His side where the soldier had hurt Him.** Point to side. **Jesus wanted His friends, the disciples, to know He was really alive. How glad they were now! Jesus was alive! They had seen Him with their own eyes.**

Jesus told them, "My Father in heaven sent Me to die for the sins of all people. Now I am sending you to go and tell others. Tell them that I died for their sins and became alive again." Then Jesus left them.

Jesus' disciples were happy. They couldn't *wait* to tell Thomas that Jesus was alive. When Thomas came, they said, "We have seen the Lord!"

But Thomas didn't believe them. Shake head no. **He said, "Unless I touch**

Key Point

We, like Thomas, doubt what we cannot see. Through His Spirit, God gives us eyes of faith that we might see Jesus in Word and Sacrament and believe in Him.

Growing in CHRisT.

Jesus' hands and side myself, I won't believe that He is alive." Point to hands and side.

The next Sunday, Jesus' disciples were all together in the same room. Again they had the doors and windows locked. Point to doors and windows. **All of a sudden, Jesus was standing in the room with them.** Look surprised. **Again He said, "Peace be with you," so they wouldn't be afraid.**

This time, Thomas was in the room too. Jesus looked at Thomas and said, "Touch the nail marks in My hands. Point to hand. **Put your hand on My side.** Point to side. **I want you to believe that I'm really alive, Thomas."**

Now Thomas believed Jesus was alive. He was so happy! He cried out to Jesus, "My Lord and my God!" Kneel, as if in front of Jesus.

Jesus said to Thomas, "You believe and are happy because you see Me. Blessed are the people who won't see Me but will still believe in Me as their Savior."

Jesus showed Thomas His hands and side. Point to hands and side. **He wanted Thomas to believe He had come alive just as He said He would. Jesus comes to us too. In our Baptism, He gives us faith to believe in Him as our Savior. Through His Word, He gives us faith to believe that He died to pay for our sins and rose again.**

Bible Story Review

What you do: You will need the leaflets and crayons. Show the picture on Lesson Leaflet 10 and use the questions to review. *Option:* Say the rhyme "Jesus Appears to Thomas" (*Wiggle & Wonder*, p. 126) with the children, or have them act out the story, playing the parts of Jesus, Thomas, and the disciples.

Ask   **Where are Jesus' friends?** They are meeting in a room.

What is Jesus doing? He is showing Thomas His hands and His side.

What does Thomas say? "My Lord and my God!"

Then hand out the leaflets, and do the sidebar activity. Younger children may want to point to the cross or tomb. Encourage them to talk about their choice. Review the story to help them discover the correct answer (hands). On side 2, have children draw crosses by all the people for whom Jesus died. Help them see that Jesus loves everyone and died for all.

Bible Words

What you do: Lead children in saying the Bible Words from John 20:29. Use the action rhyme from *Wiggle & Wonder* (© 2013 CPH) to introduce them.

Active Learning Ide

Say   Jesus showed Thomas His hands and side, and Thomas believed. God gives us faith in Jesus through Baptism and His Word, and we believe.

Say   Here is the Bible God gave me.   *Open hands like a book.*
What does He tell me? Let's look and see. *Shade hands with eyes.*
The Bible says,   *Open hands like a book.*
"Blessed are those   *Hug self.*
who have not seen   *Cover eyes.*
and yet have believed."   *Make a cross with fingers.*

③ **We Live** (20 minutes)

Help children grow in their understanding of what the Bible story means for their lives. Choose the activities that work best with your class.

Growing through God's Word

What you do: You will need Sprout. Help children begin to understand the concept of God's peace, which keeps our hearts and minds from worrying about what will happen to us because we know God loves us, forgives us for Jesus' sake, and gives us a home in heaven.

Sprout: I liked that Bible story! Thomas got a big surprise, didn't he? Jesus must have loved Thomas a lot to come back to show him He was alive.

Teacher: Yes, Sprout. Jesus loves us all very much! Jesus showed Thomas that He was alive so Thomas would believe in Him. Jesus gives us the gift of faith too! When we are baptized or hear God's Word, the Holy Spirit puts faith into our hearts. He gives us the power to believe Jesus is our Savior. The Holy Spirit also helps our faith grow when we listen to God's Word and learn more about Jesus.

Sprout: I'm glad Jesus is my Savior. Sometimes I still get scared, though.

Teacher: Yes, scary things still happen. It's not easy when moms and dads get divorces or a grandma dies. But Jesus tells us in the Bible that He is with us always. He gives us God's peace so we don't have to be afraid. He died on the cross to pay for our sins and came alive again on Easter. We can trust Him to always love and care for us.

Sprout: Teacher, are you ever afraid?

Teacher: Oh, yes! When I am afraid or worried, I read God's promises in the Bible, and I tell Jesus about my worries. You and the boys and girls can do that too, Sprout. Jesus always listens to our prayers, and He always answers in a way that is best. Let's pray now.

Pray **Dear Jesus, thank You for being our Savior. Help us always to trust in You. Give us Your peace. In Your name, we pray. Amen.**

Craft Time

What you do: Gather Craft Page 10, stickers, and crayons. For a tactile component, provide decorating supplies (e.g., raffia or snippets of yellow paper for straw, a yellow circle of sandpaper to glue to the stone, and colored tissue paper to decorate the stained glass windows).

For younger children, cut the page in half, fold both halves, and nest pages together in order ahead of time. If you have children who have trouble printing their names, make the letters of their names dot-to-dot, or use a highlighter to write the letters; then have children trace over the letters in class.

Ask **What do you believe about Jesus? How do you know these things are true? God tells us in His Word, the Bible! Today we're going to make a little book that tells things we believe about Jesus.** Show the children how to cut and assemble the booklets. Help the children write their name on their booklets, and add a sticker of Jesus to that page.

Finish the pages as follows:

1. **I believe Jesus is the Son of God.** Color straw in the manger or glue snippets of raffia or yellow paper to it.

2. **I believe Jesus loves me.** Add a Bible sticker. **The Bible tells me that Jesus loves me. He gives me parents and others to care for me.**

3. **I believe Jesus died on the cross to pay for my sins.** Color the cross and add the sticker of Jesus to it.

4. **I believe Jesus rose on Easter Day.** Add the stone sticker or sandpaper to the rolled-away stone. Color the flowers and add flower stickers.

5. **I believe Jesus answers my prayers.** Color the stained glass windows or glue on bits of colored tissue paper.

6. **I believe Jesus is always with me.** Color the picture.

7. **I believe Jesus will take me to heaven someday.** Have children draw themselves by Jesus.

Paper Plus option: Make wet-chalk pictures. Dissolve sugar in water using one part sugar to three parts water. Soak chalk in this solution for five minutes. Have the children draw pictures of Easter symbols (e.g., cross, butterfly) on paper. The sugar-water will create a different effect when pictures are dry. Rewet the chalk as needed.

Snack Time

What you do: Serve O-shaped pretzels or cereal. Talk about how they look like open mouths and how we can use our mouths to say that "Jesus is God."

Live It Out

What you do: Show children a video clip of people sharing the peace of the Lord with one another in church. Tell them we do this because God forgives us for Jesus' sake, which makes it possible for us to share His peace with others. Have them practice doing this too. They can say, "Peace of the Lord. Jesus loves you," and shake hands or hug one another.

4 Closing (5 minutes)

Going Home

What you do: Have take-home papers and crafts ready to hand out. Cue CD.

Sing "Do You Know Who Died for Me?" (*LOSP*, p. 93; CD 8). Add this stanza.

Do you know who gives me peace? Jesus does, Jesus does. Lovingly He gives me peace. Yes, He really does.

Say **God gives us His peace through Jesus.** Say take-home point together.

Pray **Thank You for dying for us and coming back to life again, Jesus. Help us to always trust in You. Amen.**

Reflection

What part of the lesson was the easiest to teach? Why? Look for similar activities for future lessons.

Preparing the Lesson

Jesus Appears in Galilee

John 21:1–19

Key Point

We are all like Peter in our words and actions, denying our Lord and weeping bitterly over what we have done. We need the same comfort Peter received—the comfort of sins forgiven and the assurance that even when we are faithless, Jesus remains faithful.

Law/**Gospel**

God demands that I love Him and none other, solely and completely. In my sin, I worship whatever pleases me most at the time. **God's love is everlasting and ever faithful; even though I deny Him, He forgives me and assures me of His love for Christ's sake.**

Context

In John's Gospel, Jesus appears to His disciples three times after His resurrection: on the actual day of resurrection (John 20:19–23); a week later, when Thomas was present (20:24–29); and here, at the Sea of Tiberias (Galilee). The event has echoes of a much earlier occasion, when Jesus called these men to be His disciples. Then as here, they caught many fish after heeding Jesus' words (Luke 5:1–7).

Commentary

On the night when Jesus was arrested and tried by the Jewish leaders, Peter three times denied that he knew Him (Matthew 26:69–75): twice to servant girls and once to some bystanders. The last time, he threw in a curse to doubly confirm his disavowal of the Master.

Peter wanted to keep his own neck out of the noose, or rather, his own hands and feet far away from Roman spikes. However, a few hours before, when Christ had predicted the betrayal, the would-be hero exclaimed, "Even if I must die with You, I will not deny You!" (Matthew 26:35). But now, loving self more than God, Peter folded under pressure.

How is Christ, now alive once more, to deal with the one who denied Him? That Peter regretted his renouncement of Jesus was evident immediately after he heard the rooster crow, for "he went out and wept bitterly" (Matthew 26:75).

But Judas, who betrayed Jesus, was also seized with remorse (27:3–4), was he not? Judas, however, despaired to the point of committing self-murder. Peter not only felt sorrow over his sin, but he also believed that the Lord would forgive him. Love, especially the love of Jesus, keeps no record of wrongs, so Peter, though full of remorse, also had faith in the absolution of the very One he had denied.

Still, how is Christ to address the situation? Shall He sweep it under the rug and never bring it up? No, that won't do. Peter needs the chance to vow that he loves Christ, just as he had thrice disavowed that love. So, using a slight variation in His questions, Jesus asks Peter, "Simon, son of John, do you love Me more than these? . . . Simon, son of John, do you love Me? . . . Simon, son of John, do you love Me?" (John 21:15, 16, 17).

After each affirmation by Peter, Jesus commands him to feed or tend His lambs and sheep—that is, to care for the Church of Christ. For the Church will be full of people like Peter, who, in their words or actions, deny their Lord, weep bitterly over what they've done, and need the same comfort that Peter received—the comfort of sins forgiven and the assurance that "if we are faithless, He [Jesus] remains faithful—for He cannot deny Himself" (2 Timothy 2:13).

To hear an in-depth discussion of this Bible account, visit cph.org/podcast and listen to our Seeds of Faith podcast each week.

Lesson 11
Jesus Appears in Galilee
John 21:1–19

Connections

Bible Words
[Jesus] is faithful and just to forgive us our sins.
1 John 1:9

Faith Word
Faithful

Hymn
All Hail the Power of Jesus' Name (*LSB* 549; CD 1)

Catechism
Office of the Keys
Confession

Take-Home Point
Jesus loves and forgives me.

1 Opening (15 minutes)

Welcome Time

What you do: Before class, set up two activity areas. In one, put out copies of Activity Page 11 and crayons. Make copies of Activity Page Fun (below and on CD) for parents or classroom helpers. Adjust talk as necessary.

In the other area, set out play dough, fish cookie cutters, and a variety of buttons. *Option:* Use a tablet device. Set out cornmeal in a bowl or cookie sheet.

Play the CD from your Teacher Tools. Greet children and give them a sticker to put on the attendance chart, and show them where to put their offering.

Say Hi, [Antoine]. I'm glad to see you! I wonder . . . have you ever gone fishing? Today you'll hear about a time Jesus' disciples were fishing.

Direct children to the tables where you have the activities. Encourage parents or caregivers to stay and do the welcome activity with their child.

Activity Page Fun Get a copy of the Activity Page to show your child.

Ask What is happening in this picture? Let child tell. **There is something hidden in this picture. Look carefully. What is it?** Have child look for hidden hearts. **Hearts remind us of love. The Bible story today is about Jesus' love and forgiveness. Whom do you think Jesus loves in this picture?** (Everyone) **Draw crosses on them to show that Jesus loves them so much that He died on the cross for them.**

MATERIALS NEEDED

1 Opening	2 God Speaks	3 We Live	4 Closing
Teacher Tools Attendance chart CD	**Teacher Tools** Poster D	**Student Pack** Craft Page 11 Stickers	**Teacher Tools** CD
Student Pack Attendance sticker	**Student Pack** Lesson Leaflet 11	**Other Supplies** Heart & fish pictures Cross	**Student Pack** Take-home items
Other Supplies Activity Page 11 (TG) Play dough & fish cookie cutters Buttons Dish with cornmeal (optional) Resource Page 1 (TG)	**Other Supplies** Easel, chalkboard, or desk Poster paper Paper cups Shoebox Netting or plastic bag & paper fish	Yarn Decorating supplies Paper Plus supplies (optional) Fish crackers or bread, jam & fish cookie cutters	

Active Learning Children can use the cookie cutters to make fish. Also, show them how to shape the play dough into a football shape for the body of the fish and a triangle for the tail. Encourage the children to make big fish and little fish and to count their fish. Give them buttons to decorate their fish.

For kindergarten-age children, set out a tablet device with the Hungry Fish app by Motion Math on it, or find a similar app. Set the app to the appropriate level for the age of your children, and show them how to drag the bubbles to feed the hungry fish. Encourage collaboration.

Say   In our Bible story today, Jesus' disciples are fishing.

Option: Put cornmeal in a baking dish or on a cookie sheet. Show children how to make a curved line for half a fish. Then, show them how to make a second curved line to complete the fish.

Say   Christians used to draw fish this way to show they were Jesus' followers. Today, we will hear a Bible story about Jesus and fish and Jesus' love.

Use your classroom signal to let the children know when it is time to clean up. Sing a cleanup song (Resource Page 1). Have children pretend to be fish and swim over to your story area.

Gathering in God's Name

What you do: Begin with this opening. To teach about the Church Year, use the materials in the Church Year Worship Kit (see the introduction).

Say   Hi, boys and girls! I'm glad you are here today! Let's sing.

Sing   "God Loves Me Dearly" (*LOSP*, p. 85; CD 9) or "All Hail the Power of Jesus' Name" (*LSB* 549; CD 1)

Invite the children to say the Invocation and Amen with you. Tell them "Amen" is the special word we say to ask Jesus to hear our prayers just like He promised.

Begin   In the name of the Father and of the Son and of the Holy Spirit. Amen.

Offering   Have a child bring the offering basket forward. Sing an offering song. Pause at asterisks (*) and have children echo each phrase in the prayer. Tell children you will say a phrase and then they can pray it back to God.

Pray   Dear Jesus,* thank You* for dying on the cross* to pay for our sins.* We are happy* You rose again on Easter!* We are happy* we can live with You in heaven.* Amen.*

Celebrate   Birthdays, Baptism birthdays, and special occasions

 **2 God Speaks** (20 minutes)

Story Clue

What you do: Have large pieces of paper and an easel or something to rest the paper against so the children can see what you are drawing.

Say   Our story today from God's Word has two things in it. Draw a simple fish (football body and triangle tail) on the paper.

Ask   What does this look like? Yes, a fish. Our story today has fish in it. Draw a large heart as the children watch. **What is this? Yes, it's a heart.**

Say   Sometimes, when people see a heart, they think about love. Our story today is also about love. It sounds funny to have a story about fish and love, doesn't it? But that's what it's about. In the story, Jesus uses some fish to show His disciples who He is. But most important, our Bible story is about love—Jesus' love for Peter and His love for all of us.

Bible Story Time

What you do: You will need Poster D. Draw faces on paper cups to represent Jesus, Peter, and a few disciples. Draw a simple boat on a shoebox to represent the boat. Attach netting or a large plastic bag to the "boat" for the fish net. Fill it with plastic or paper fish. Use the fish outline on this page to make lots of fish, or draw your own fish by drawing a football and adding a triangle on the end for a tail. *Option:* Find an audio clip of water lapping at a boat.

Say   After Easter, before Jesus went back to His home in heaven, Jesus went to see His friends on earth. One day, early in the morning, Jesus went to the Sea of Galilee. Jesus' friends, the disciples, were out in their boat. Play audio clip. **All night long they had tried to catch some fish, but they didn't catch even one! Jesus called, "Have you caught anything?"**

The friends didn't know it was Jesus. They answered, "No! Not one fish!"

Then, Jesus said, "Throw your net on the other side of the boat and try again." So, they threw their net over that side of the boat. Guess what happened? They caught so many fish in their fishing net that they couldn't lift it out of the water! When John saw all the fish, he knew that the person on the shore had to be Jesus. He told Peter, "It's Jesus!"

Now Peter was excited! He jumped into the water and swam to the shore. The disciples followed in their boat, towing the net full of fish.

Jesus was cooking fish over a fire on the beach. Jesus told His friends, "Come and eat with Me." So, they all sat down and ate breakfast together. They were so happy to see Jesus and know that He was really alive. Jesus had changed their long, tiring night into a happy time.

After they were done eating, Jesus talked to Peter. Remember, just a few weeks ago on the night before Jesus died, Peter had told people three times that he didn't know Jesus.

Ask   How do you think Peter felt when he did this? Accept answers.

Say   Peter was sorry he had lied about knowing Jesus. But Jesus loved Peter and forgave him. He paid for our sins on the cross. Now Jesus had special work for Peter to do. Show Poster D. **Jesus asked Peter, "Do you love Me?"**

Peter answered, "Yes, Lord, You know I love You!"

Jesus said, "Feed My lambs."

Jesus asked Peter the same question a second time: "Do you truly love Me?"

Peter answered, "Yes, Lord."

Jesus said, "Take care of My sheep." A third time, Jesus asked, "Simon

Key Point

We are all like Peter in our words and actions, denying our Lord and weeping bitterly over what we have done. We need the same comfort Peter received—the comfort of sins forgiven and the assurance that even when we are faithless, Jesus remains faithful.

Peter, do you love Me?"

Peter told Jesus for the third time, "Lord, You know everything. You know that I love You."

This time Jesus said, "Feed My sheep!"

Peter sinned, but Jesus forgave him. Then, He gave Peter a job to do. He told Peter to feed His sheep. Peter knew that Jesus wasn't asking him to take care of sheep but to take care of people. Jesus wanted Peter to tell people that Jesus came to be our Savior from sin.

We think and say and do wrong things too. We sin. But Jesus came to be our Savior. We can trust Jesus to love and forgive us, no matter what.

Bible Story Review

What you do: You will need the Lesson Leaflets and crayons or markers. First, show Poster D. Ask these questions to review:

Ask Who helped the disciples catch many fish? Jesus

What does Jesus want Peter to know? That He forgives Peter

What does Jesus want Peter to do? He wants Peter to "feed His sheep"—to tell people that He loves them and died to pay for their sins.

Hand out the leaflets and crayons. On side 1, have children circle the fish and draw a cross over Peter. On side 2, show them how to make an oval shape with crisscross lines for a fish net.

Option: Assign roles for Jesus, Peter, John, and the other disciples. Retell the Bible story, having the children pretend they are the various characters in it. Or, use this action rhyme to review the story. Have the children join in the actions and supply the answers in their own words.

Active Learning Id

Say Peter said, "I'm going fishing." *Stand up and walk in place.*
The disciples said, "We'll go too!" *Motion with hand.*
So, into the boat they climbed. Then, they said, *Crouch down.*
"Throw out the nets; let's see what the fish will do." *Throw a net.*
All night long, they watched and waited. *Put hand over eyes as if looking.*
Not one fish swam into their net. *Shake head no.*
Then, someone shouted, "Catch any fish?" *Cup hands around mouth.*
They shook their heads no. "We haven't caught one yet." *Shake head no.*
"Throw your nets on the other side," the man said. *Throw nets.*
When they did, their nets were filled with fish. *Pull in nets.*
John cried out, "It's Jesus!" Then, Peter swam to the shore! *"Swim."*
Jesus was cooking fish to eat; it was a tasty dish. *"Eat."*
Later, Jesus asked, "Peter, do you love Me?" *Children answer yes.*
Peter, sorry for his sins, said, "Yes, Lord, You know I do." *Nod head.*
Jesus answered, "Follow Me; tell others of My love. *Spread arms wide.*
I died for everyone's sins. I love you and you and you." *Point to children.*

Bible Words

What you do: Read 1 John 1:9 from your Bible: "[Jesus] is faithful and just to forgive us our sins." Lead children in saying the Bible Words using an action rhyme from *Wiggle & Wonder* (© 2013 CPH).

Say Here is the Bible God gave me. *Open hands like a book.*
What does He tell me? Let's look and see. *Shade hands with eyes.*

The Bible says,	Hold hands like open book.
"[Jesus]	Point to "nail hole" in each palm.
is faithful and just	Put one fist on top of the other.
to forgive us	Make cross with fingers.
our sins."	Cross arms over chest.

Jesus loved Peter and forgave his sins. He gave Peter a special job to do. Jesus loves and cares for us too. He forgives our sins. Say Bible Words again.

3 We Live (20 minutes)

Help children grow in their understanding of what the Bible story means for their lives. Choose the activities that work best with your class.

Growing through God's Word

What you do: Use the pictures of a heart and fish that you drew earlier. Have paper to draw a cross, or bring a cross to show.

Say Before I told the Bible story today, I drew two things. What did I draw? Accept answers. **I drew a fish and a heart. I said our story would be about fish and love.** Show heart. **This heart reminds us of Jesus' love.** Show fish. **The fish reminds us of how Jesus cares for us and gives us what we need.**

Ask How did Jesus show His love and care in the Bible story? (Jesus showed His love for His disciples. He filled their nets with fish. He cooked fish for them to eat.) **Jesus takes care of us each day too.**

What are some ways that Jesus shows His love and care for us? (He gives us our family and a place to live. He gives us food and clothing and all the things we need.)

Say Let's say, "Thank You, Jesus!" together. Do so. Draw or hold up cross. **Most of all, our story is about Jesus' forgiveness. Jesus forgave Peter and gave him an important job to do. Jesus forgives us too. Jesus loves us so much that He came to take the punishment for all the wrong things we think and say and do. He did this by dying on the cross and coming back to life again.**

Ask Can you make the sign of the cross to show that Jesus died for you? Do so.

Say Jesus loves you and died for your sins. You can make the sign of the cross whenever you want to remember God's love for you.

Craft Time

What you do: Use Craft Page 11, stickers, markers or crayons, yarn, and decorating supplies to finish the fish and card. *Option:* Cut the fish section off ahead of time.

Say When Jesus' disciples saw all the fish in their net, they knew only God's Son, Jesus, could make something like that happen. It was a miracle. After Jesus went back to His home in heaven, the people who believed in Him used a fish to show others they believed in Jesus. One Christian would draw half a fish in the dirt or on walls. Draw the first curved line of the fish symbol on paper. **If the person watching was a Christian, the person would finish the fish.** Draw second curved line. **The fish picture was a symbol or a sign for being a follower of Jesus.**

Show fish cut from Craft Page. **We're going to make a fish necklace to show that we believe in Jesus.** Let children decorate fish. Add a piece of yarn to the fish to make a necklace.

Read the words on the remaining section. **This card says, "Jesus loves you and cares for you." You can draw a picture on the card and add some decorations to it.**

Give the children a Jesus sticker to add to the front. They can color the heart and child and use the remaining stickers and other decorating items to personalize their cards. Ask your pastor to give these cards to shut-ins or the sick.

Paper Plus option: Make fish place mats. Find a simple fish pattern online, or enlarge the fish on Craft Page 11, and trace around it onto a large piece of construction paper. Give the children google eyes, markers, pieces of tissue paper or foil wrapping paper, and other decorating supplies to finish their fish. Make copies of a table prayer to glue to the place mat.

Snack Time

What you do: Serve fish crackers or a piece of bread with jam. Cut a fish shape with a cookie cutter.

Live It Out

What you do: Encourage children to give the cards they made to people who are sick or old and can't come to church to remind them that Jesus loves them and cares for them.

4 Closing (5 minutes)

Going Home

What you do: Have leaflets and crafts ready to hand out. Cue CD.

Say **Jesus showed love when He filled the disciples' nets with fish. He showed love for Peter when He forgave him and gave him a special job. Jesus is faithful and just. He loves and forgives us too.** Say take-home point together.

Sing "I'm in God's Family" (*S&W*, p. 58; CD 10)

Pray **Dear Jesus, thank You* for loving us,* for forgiving us,* for caring about us,* and for making us* Your children. Amen.** Pause at each asterisk (*) and have children echo each phrase.

Reflection

How does Sunday School provide love and care for families? Assure the children of Jesus' love and forgiveness for them. They can't hear it too often!

Color the hidden hearts. How many are there?

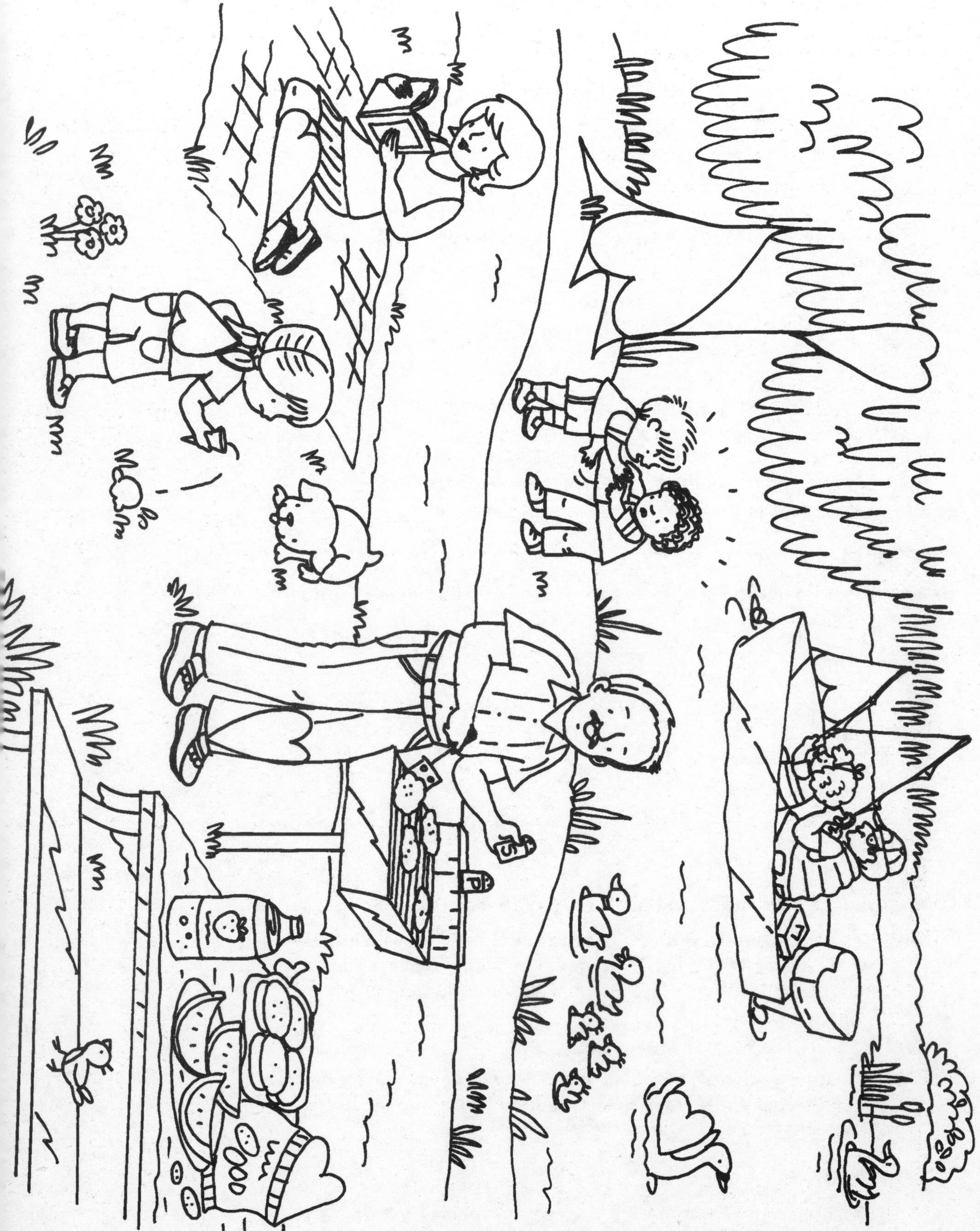

Preparing the Lesson

Jesus Ascends into Heaven

Acts 1:1–11; Luke 24:44–53

Date of Use

Key Point

Jesus, our risen Savior, ascended to heaven to prepare a place for us there with Him.

Law/**Gospel**

I sin when I live as if the ascended Christ is no longer active in my life and the world. **Jesus ascended into heaven to prepare an eternal home for me, and I can trust His promise to be with me now and always.**

Context

After He died and rose again, Jesus taught His disciples for forty days. John indicates that the disciples understood things only *after* Jesus rose again (see John 12:16), and Luke says that Jesus spoke about "the kingdom of God" (Acts 1:3). Jesus' ascension also looks forward to the coming of the Holy Spirit on Pentecost (Acts 2).

Commentary

Luke connects his Book of Acts back to his "first book," the Gospel of Luke. The disciples heard Jesus' teachings and witnessed His miraculous works, especially His bloody death and glorious resurrection. Now Jesus gives His final teachings before He returns to the Father (Acts 1:3–5).

Not only does Jesus teach the disciples about the purpose of His life and work—namely, that He came to forgive sinners by dying and rising for them—but He also prepares them to receive "the promise of the Father," that is, the Holy Spirit Himself (Acts 1:4).

Before Jesus ascends, He commissions His eleven disciples to be His witnesses (Acts 1:8). The Book of Acts demonstrates how the Holy Spirit works through the preaching of Christ and Him crucified to make the Church grow and flourish.

As Jesus ascended, "a cloud took Him out of their sight" (Acts 1:9), and two angels appeared and asked the disciples why they were looking up into heaven. Jesus' Church does not live by sight, but rather by faithfully hearing His Word.

When He ascends, Jesus does not leave His Church (see Matthew 28:20). He may no longer be visibly present, but He is very much present in the baptizing and teaching (Matthew 28:19–20), in the preaching of the Gospel (Mark 16:15), in the forgiving of sins (John 20:23), and in the breaking of the bread (see Luke 24:30, 35).

In Luke 24:44–53, Luke tells us some of the things that Jesus taught His disciples during the forty days prior to His ascension. He taught the disciples that all of Scripture points to Him (v. 44) and that the Church, especially through the Office of the Ministry, proclaims "repentance and forgiveness of sins . . . to all nations" (Luke 24:47).

The Church does not make up or periodically change her message, because Jesus gave the message to her. The Church proclaims Christ crucified and risen as the beating heart of the Scriptures. The Holy Spirit enables the Church and her ministers to proclaim repentance for the forgiveness of sins throughout the world.

After Jesus ascended, the disciples "returned to Jerusalem with great joy, and were continually in the temple," the place of worship (Luke 24:52–53). They knew and trusted that the Lord Jesus was still with them, and they wanted to remain in His presence in the Holy Place.

To hear an in-depth discussion of this Bible account, visit cph.org/podcast and listen to our Seeds of Faith podcast each week.

Lesson 12
Jesus Ascends into Heaven
Acts 1:1–11; Luke 24:44–53

Connections

Bible Words
[Jesus says,] "I am with you always."
Matthew 28:20 (CD 5)

Faith Words
Ascend, Ascension

Hymn
All Hail the Power of Jesus' Name
(*LSB* 549; CD 1)

Catechism
Apostles' Creed:
Second Article

Liturgy
Apostles' Creed

Take-Home Point
Jesus is with me always.

1 Opening (15 minutes)

Welcome Time

What you do: Before class, set up two activity areas. In one, put out copies of Activity Page 12A and crayons. Make copies of Activity Page Fun (below and on CD) for parents or classroom helpers. Adjust talk as necessary.

In the other area, cover a table with a plastic tablecloth or set out cookie sheets at each place setting. Have shaving cream to squirt on the tablecloth or cookie sheets. Also, set out play dough and angel cookie cutters. *Option:* Set out suitcases, dress-up clothes, purses, wallets, play money, and old maps.

Play the CD from your Teacher Tools. Greet children and give them a sticker to put on the attendance chart, and show them where to put their offering.

Say Hi, [Layla]. I'm glad to see you! I wonder . . . do you like to look at the clouds and find shapes in them? Today, we'll talk more about clouds.

Direct children to the tables where you have the activities. Encourage parents or caregivers to stay and do the welcome activity with their child.

Activity Page Fun Get a copy of the Activity Page to show your child.

Say Animals and people have homes. Fish live in water. Birds build nests. Where do people live? Accept answers. **Draw a line to match these animals and children to the place they live. Right now you live at home with [name people in your family]. In the Bible story today, Jesus goes back to His home in heaven. He tells us that He is going there to get a special place ready for us. Listen carefully so you can tell me what you learn today.**

MATERIALS NEEDED

1 Opening	2 God Speaks	3 We Live	4 Closing
Teacher Tools Attendance chart & CD	**Teacher Tools** Storytelling Figures 12-1 to 12-6 Background A CD	**Student Pack** Craft Page 12 Stickers	**Teacher Tools** CD
Student Pack Attendance sticker	**Student Pack** Lesson Leaflet 12 Stickers	**Other Supplies** Activity Page 12B (TG) Cotton balls	**Student Pack** Take-home materials

Other Supplies
Activity Page 12A (TG)
Cookie sheets or plastic table-
    cloth & shaving cream
Play dough, angel cookie cutters
Dress-up items
Resource Page 1 (TG)
	Other Supplies
	Jesus Returns to Heaven Arch
	    Book (optional)
	Cotton balls
		Travel items in a bag
		Toy car or picture of a car
		Colored paper
		Paper Plus supplies & Activity Page
		    12C (optional)
		Marshmallows or pudding	

Active Learning Squirt shaving cream on the table or cookie sheets. Let the children make clouds. At another table, give them play dough and cookie cutters to cut out angel shapes.

Say **You are making angels and clouds. You will hear about them today.**

Option: Line up chairs for a pretend airplane, train, or bus. Have children use the dress-up items to pretend they are taking a trip. Ask them where they are going and what they might see. Remind them that Jesus promises in His Word that He is with us no matter where we go.

Use your classroom signal to let the children know when it is time to clean up. Sing a cleanup song (Resource Page 1). Have children pretend to drive a car and drive over to the story area.

Gathering in God's Name

What you do: Begin with this opening. To teach about the Church Year, use the materials in the Church Year Worship Kit (see the introduction).

Say **Hi, boys and girls! Are you ready to sing a Jesus song?**
Sing "Jesus Ascends" (*S&W*, p. 41; CD 11) or "All Hail the Power of Jesus' Name" (*LSB* 549; CD 1)

Invite the children to say the Invocation with you. Tell them "Amen" is the special word we say to ask Jesus to hear our prayers just like He promised.

Begin **In the name of the Father and of the Son and of the Holy Spirit. Amen.**
Offering Have a child bring the offering basket forward. Sing an offering song.

Pray **Dear Jesus, thank You for loving us. Thank You for dying on the cross for our sins and for coming alive again. Thank You for listening to our prayers. We pray for** (include children's prayer requests)**. In Jesus' name we pray. Amen.**
Celebrate Birthdays, Baptism birthdays, and special occasions

11, 1

Liturgy Link
Each time we say the Apostles' Creed during a worship service, we say, "He ascended into heaven." Talk about what this phrase means with the children, and practice saying it together. Encourage them to listen for it and say it with the grown-ups in church.

2 God Speaks (20 minutes)

Story Clue

What you do: No supplies are needed.

Ask **Boys and girls, when your grandma and grandpa come for a visit and then say, "It's time for us to go home," do you feel sad? Do you wave good-bye to them? When you're playing at a friend's house and it's time to go home, do you sometimes wish you could stay longer? Our Bible story today tells about the time Jesus left the earth to go back to His home in heaven.**

Bible Story Time

What you do: Use Storytelling Figures 12-1 to 12-6 and Background A. Use a restickable glue stick, double-sided tape, or loops of tape to attach the figures. Remind the children that this is a true story from the Bible. *Option:* Tell the story using the Arch Book *Jesus Returns to Heaven* (CPH, 59-1561)

Say God sent His Son, Jesus, from heaven to be our Savior. Jesus was born as a little baby. He grew up and taught people about God's love. Add Jesus (12-1). **He healed people who were sick. He fed people who were hungry. He suffered and died on the cross to take away our sins. Then He came alive again on Easter. For many days after Easter, Jesus visited and talked to people to show them He was alive. Jesus wanted everyone to know that He was the Savior God promised to send. Now Jesus' work on earth was done, and it was time for Him to go back to His heavenly home.**

Before He left them, Jesus took His friends the disciples up a hill. Add disciples (12-2). **Jesus told them that He still loved them and would be with them always. He told them that it was now their job to tell about God's love and what Jesus had done for them.**

He said, "Go everywhere and tell people about Me. Tell them that I died on the cross to take away their sins. Tell them that I came alive again at Easter. Baptize people in the name of the Father and the Son and the Holy Spirit. And remember that I am with you always." Then He told them that He was sending them the Holy Spirit to help them do God's work on earth.

As Jesus was talking, He began to ascend into the sky. Replace 12-1 with figure of Jesus ascending (12-3). ***Ascend* means "to go up." Up, up, up, Jesus went.** Look up toward ceiling. **Jesus' friends watched Him go up into the sky. But soon a cloud came and covered Jesus up.** Add cloud (12-4) over Jesus. **They couldn't see Him anymore! Jesus had gone to His home in heaven.**

All of a sudden, two angels stood in white robes beside Jesus' friends. Add angels (12-5 and 12-6), one on either side of the disciples (12-2). **Do you think Jesus' friends were surprised? Show me your surprised face. The angels asked Jesus' friends, "Why are you standing here looking up in the sky? Someday Jesus will come back, and you will see Him again."**

Then the friends went back to the city to wait for the Holy Spirit to come. They couldn't see Jesus, but they knew He would be with them always, just as He had promised. They knew that Jesus would send the Holy Spirit to help them do His work on earth. They knew that someday they would see Him again. And someday they would live with Him in a beautiful place called heaven.

Jesus is with us too. He washes away our sins in Baptism. He gives us the Holy Spirit to help us live as His children. He speaks to us through His Word. Someday we will live with Him in heaven too.

Key Point

Jesus, our risen Savior, ascended to heaven to prepare a place for us there with Him.

Bible Story Review

What you do: You will need Lesson Leaflet 12, stickers, crayons, cotton balls, and glue sticks. Show Lesson Leaflet 12. Ask these questions to review:

Ask **What is Jesus doing?** Ascending into the sky to go back to heaven

What did Jesus say He would do in heaven? Get a place ready for us

Will Jesus come back again? Yes.

Is Jesus still with us now? Yes. He promised, "I am with you always."

Hand out the leaflets and crayons. Give children stickers of a disciple and

Growing in CHRIST

Jesus' face to add to the sidebar pictures. Have the children color the cloud or glue pulled-apart cotton balls to it. On the back of the page, have the children circle and color all the places Jesus is with them.

Bible Words

What you do: Read the Bible Words from Matthew 28:20 in the Bible and listen to them on the CD. Do the litany with the children to reinforce the words.

Say **Jesus left earth and went back to heaven, but He promised His friends, "I am with you always." Can you say Jesus' words with me?** Say the Bible Words a few times. **Now let's sing them.** Play track 5 on the CD.

We can't see Jesus, but He promises to be with us too. In our Baptism, Jesus makes us His children. Through His Word, Jesus talks to us. He tells us that He forgives our sins. When we have troubles, we can remember His promise: "I am with you always."

Help the children say the Bible Words after each situation you name. Vary the situations to the needs of the children in your class.

Say **When something makes you afraid, you can remember . . .**
Children's response: [Jesus says,] "I am with you always."
When you are playing, you can remember . . . Response
When you are sick and pray to Jesus, you can remember . . . Response
Jesus loves you. He does not leave you alone. He is with you always.

3 We Live (20 minutes)

Help children grow in their understanding of what the Bible story means for their lives. Choose the activities that work best with your class.

Growing through God's Word

What you do: Put a few items you would use on a trip in an overnight bag. Also, have a picture of a car or a small toy car. Enlarge and copy the pictures on Activity Page 12B. Cut them apart, and tape them to pieces of colored paper. *Option:* Show pictures of vacation spots on your tablet device or phone.

Ask Hold up bag. **What do you think I have inside my bag?** Accept replies. Take out the items to show the children. **I packed these things because I'm going to visit a friend for a few days. Do you think Jesus will know where I am?** Wait for their replies. **I'm going to drive in my car for a few hours to get there.** Show a picture of a car, or hold up a toy car. **Will Jesus know that I'm in my car? Will He watch over me when I'm away from home?** Wait for their replies.

Say **We can't see Jesus. But we know He is with us always. He tells us this in the Bible. Jesus is God, so He has power to do what He says. He always keeps His promises. No matter where we go or what we do, Jesus promises He is there. That makes me so happy! It means we can talk to Jesus.**

Ask **How do we do that?** Accept responses. **Yes, we talk to Jesus when we pray.** Show picture of praying child. **Jesus hears and answers our prayers in a way that is best for us. Does Jesus talk to us too? How?**

Say **Jesus talks to us in His Word, the Bible.** Show picture of family in church listening to pastor reading Bible. **He tells us that He loves us so much that He died on the cross to pay for our sins. He tells us to share His love with others. He wants all people to hear about Him and believe in Him.**

Ask **What is happening in this picture?** Show picture of two children fighting. **Does Jesus see us when we sin?** Accept answers.

Say **Yes, Jesus is always with us. He knows when we are sinning. Jesus does not want us to sin. But do you know what?** Draw a large cross over the picture. **Jesus paid for all our sins on the cross. When we were baptized, the pastor made a cross over us to show that Jesus paid for our sins on the cross. Jesus helps us to feel sorry for the wrong things we do. He helps us say, "I'm sorry; please forgive me."**

Ask **What does Jesus do then? He forgives us! Jesus helps us to forgive others, too, when they hurt us.**

Say **Jesus helps us to show love and tell others about His love.** Point to the picture of children forgiving each other. **Jesus is always with us.**

Have the children stand and echo your words at the asterisks.

Say **Jesus loves me.* Jesus takes care of me.***
Jesus is with me* everywhere I go.*
I'll be with Jesus* in heaven one day.*

Craft Time

What you do: You will need Craft Page 12, stickers, crayons, cotton balls, and glue. To make the project, first cut off the strip with Jesus on it. Fold the remaining part of the page in half so the solid lines in the middle of the page are on the fold. Cut along these two lines. When you open the page, you will have two slits in the middle of the scene. Insert the Jesus strip from the bottom of the page behind the hill and pull it through the first slit, over the sky background, and through the second slit under the cloud. See diagram.

Help the children assemble the ascension scene according to the directions. Have Jesus visible. *Note:* Preassemble the projects for young children and those with special needs, or cut off the Jesus figure and help the children glue it in place on their background scene.

Say **Here is a picture of Jesus with His disciples.** Show children how to pull the blue side of the strip to make Jesus disappear under the cloud. **Where is Jesus going? Yes, He is going back to His home in heaven. Someday we will live with Him in heaven.** Give children cotton balls to glue to the clouds and angel stickers to put on side 1.

Ask **What did Jesus promise His disciples before He went back to heaven? Yes, Jesus said, "I am with you always."** Turn the page over. Leave the strip in, but hide Jesus so only the Bible and baptismal font show. **Can you see Jesus now? No. Is Jesus still with us? Yes. How do we know? Jesus is God. He has all power. He keeps His promises.**

Say **In Baptism, Jesus makes us His children.** Point to baptismal font. **Jesus tells us in the Bible that He is with us.** Point to Bible and read the words on it. Have children color water and add stickers of shell and cross near font.

Let's look at some of the places where Jesus is with us. Is Jesus with us

Growing in CHRiST.

when we play? Yes. Pull strip to reveal Jesus. **Trace the line from Jesus to the boy and girl playing. Jesus is with us when we are playing.**

Move strip to cover Jesus again. Point to picture of child sleeping in bed. **Is Jesus with us when we are asleep in our beds? Yes.** Make Jesus appear again. **Trace the line from Jesus to the child sleeping. Jesus is with us when we are sleeping.** Children can color the blanket squares. Talk about how Jesus is with us in the remaining scenes, and have the children connect Jesus to what is pictured. Then, have children hide Jesus again. **We can't see Jesus anymore because He went back to heaven.**

Ask **How do we know He is with us?** Wait for replies.

Say **He gives us His Word, the Bible** (point to Bible on picture strip)**, so that He can talk to us and tell us that He loves us. He gives us Holy Baptism** (point to baptismal font) **to tell us that He loves us and forgives our sins.**

Whenever we are afraid or wonder if Jesus is with us, we can hear Him talk to us in His Word and remember His promise. Lead children in saying Bible words again. **[Jesus says,] "I am with you always." One day, everyone who believes in Jesus will see Him again in heaven.**

Paper Plus option: Make copies of Activity Page 12C. Have children color their page and glue pulled-apart cotton balls to it for clouds. Optionally, have them pretend they were there with disciples and draw themselves watching Jesus ascend. Glue the picture to a piece of construction paper for a "frame" effect. String with yarn to hang.

Snack Time

What you do: Serve small marshmallows or pudding to remind the children of clouds. Avoid large marshmallows, as they can be a choking hazard.

Live It Out

What you do: Encourage children to give their Ascension picture to a friend or family member and tell the person today's Bible story.

 **4 Closing** (5 minutes)

14, 11

Going Home

What you do: Have leaflets and crafts ready to hand out. Cue CD.

Say **Today you heard the story of Jesus' ascension into heaven. Jesus is preparing a place for us there. But He hasn't left us alone. He promises He is with us always. Let's say, "Jesus is with me always" together.** Do so.

Sing "Jesus Loves Me" (*LOSP*, p. 42; CD 14) or "Jesus Ascends" (*S&W*, p. 41; CD 11) again

Pray **Dear Jesus, thank You for coming to earth to be our Savior and going back to heaven to prepare a wonderful home for us. Amen.**

Reflection

Did the children find comfort in knowing that Jesus is present with them in all situations? Did they begin to grasp that we can have this certainty because of Jesus' promise in His Word and our Baptism?

Draw a line to match these animals and children to the place where they live.

Where is your home?

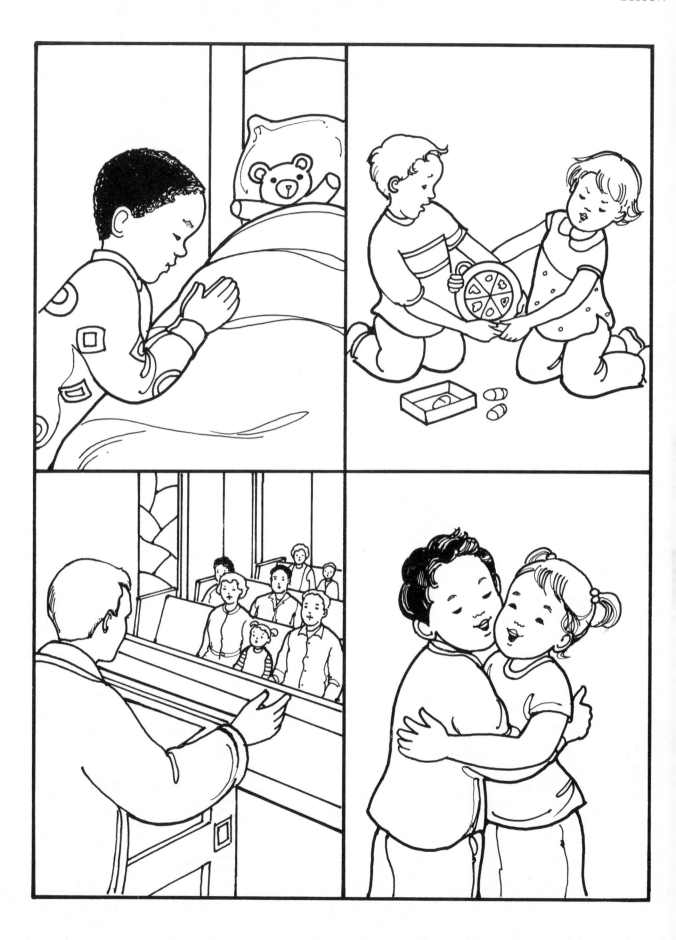

Jesus Ascends into Heaven

Lesson 13

Preparing the Lesson

John's Vision of Heaven

Revelation 21–22

Date of Use

Key Point

Those who believe that salvation has been accomplished by the all-availing sacrifice of Jesus on the cross will bear the sign of Christ, written on their forehead in Holy Baptism, and they will have access to the tree of life.

Law/Gospel

If I do not believe in Christ as my Savior, I will not enter the gates of heaven. **I am baptized and believe in Jesus, the Lamb of God; He has written my name in His Book of Life. Someday, I will live with Him in the new heavenly Jerusalem, where there will be no more sorrow or pain or death.**

Context

This is the acme of John's Revelation, indeed, the climax of all the Scriptures. In many ways, it is also a digest or summary of the Bible, for these two chapters contain the teachings of sin and salvation, heaven and hell, Jesus and the Church, the Holy Trinity, and so forth. John plucks images, as if flowers, from various other books of both the Old Testament and New Testament to weave this textual bouquet that pictures the inheritance of the saints.

Commentary

The Church walks into the future facing backward. She sees *what will be* by gazing toward *what was*, for the end is a replica of the beginning, only better. For that reason, heaven is not pictured as a golf course or Candyland but as a new Eden and new Jerusalem.

As the garden home of our first parents had the tree of life and a river flowing out of it (Genesis 2:9–10), so the celestial Eden has "the river of the water of life, bright as crystal, flowing from the throne of God and of the Lamb through the middle of the street of the city" and "on either side of the river, the tree of life with its twelve kinds of fruit, yielding its fruit each month" (Revelation 22:1–2).

As Jerusalem was the city where God dwelt among His people through much of Israel's history, so the "holy city, new Jerusalem" comes down out of heaven from God with the announcement: "Behold, the dwelling place of God is with man" (21:2–3). But whereas in the old Jerusalem, the Lord was housed in His sanctuary, in the new Jerusalem, there is no temple structure, for the city's temple "is the Lord God the Almighty and the Lamb" (21:22). Indeed, Christ is "making all things new" (21:5).

This is not a utopia open to everyone, however. Excluded are those who are unclean (21:27)—that is, who have not "washed their robes and made them white in the blood of the Lamb" (7:14). Sinners are not excluded from heaven for breaking the Law but for breaking the Gospel. They refuse to believe that "it is done" (21:6), that salvation has been accomplished by the all-availing sacrifice of Jesus' body and blood on the cross.

Those who believe, however, will have the name of Christ written on their forehead with the pen of Holy Baptism (22:4). They are the children of God (21:7), those who, thirsting for righteousness, drink "from the spring of the water of life without payment" (21:6). They have "the right to the tree of life and . . . they may enter the city by the gates" (22:14), the city they shall forever call home.

To hear an in-depth discussion of this Bible account, visit cph.org/podcast and listen to our Seeds of Faith podcast each week.

Lesson 13
John's Vision of Heaven
Revelation 21–22

Connections

Bible Words
[God] desires all people to be saved. 1 Timothy 2:4

Faith Word
Heaven

Hymn
All Hail the Power of Jesus' Name (*LSB* 549; CD 1)

Catechism
Apostles' Creed

Liturgy
Apostles' Creed: Third Article

Take-Home Point
Jesus gives all those who believe in Him a home in heaven.

(1) Opening (15 minutes)

Welcome Time

What you do: Before class, set up two activity areas. In one, put out copies of Activity Page 13A and crayons or markers. Also set out small, brightly colored decorative items, such as snips of metallic paper, flat buttons, or plastic "jewels" and glue sticks. Make copies of Activity Page Fun (below and on CD) for parents or classroom helpers. Adjust talk as necessary.

In the other area, set out pictures of mountains, farms, forests, and the like. Also have some pictures of places that preschoolers would like to visit, such as the zoo, a circus, or an amusement park. *Option:* Search for pictures online to show on your tablet device.

Play the CD from your Teacher Tools. Greet children and give them a sticker to put on the attendance chart, and show them where to put their offering.

Say Hi, [Isaac]. I'm glad to see you! What is a special place you like to go? Today, we'll hear about a special place the Bible talks about.

Activity Page Fun Get a copy of the Activity Page to show your child. Tell your child to look for the happy faces hidden in the picture.

Say There are some happy faces hidden in this picture. Let's look for them and count them. Help your child find the faces. Then, color the picture with your child and add jewel-like decorations. Comment on the picture when it is complete. **In the Bible story today, you will hear about a beautiful city and find out why the people there are so happy.**

MATERIALS NEEDED

1 Opening	2 God Speaks	3 We Live	4 Closing
Teacher Tools Attendance chart CD	**Teacher Tools** Posters E & F CD	**Student Pack** Craft Page 13 Stickers	**Teacher Tools** CD

Student Pack
Attendance sticker
	Student Pack
	Lesson Leaflet 13
		Other Supplies
		Beanbag or beanbag animal
		Activity Page 13B & Paper Plus
		   supplies (optional)
		Angel cookies or bread, cream
		   cheese & angel cookie cutters
			Student Pack
			Take-home items

Other Supplies Activity Page 13A (TG) Small jewels & other decorations Pictures of beautiful or fun places Resource Page 1 (TG)	**Other Supplies** Blank paper		

Active Learning Spread out the pictures you collected on a table and let the children look at them, or show pictures on your tablet device of beautiful scenery or fun places children like to go.

Ask **Which of these pictures looks like a place that you would like to visit? Why would you like to go there? What would you do?**

Say **There are some beautiful and fun places in the world. But God made someplace that is more beautiful and more wonderful than any of these places in the pictures. That place is called heaven, the place we will live with Jesus someday. In today's lesson, we will learn more about heaven.**

Use your classroom signal to let the children know when it is time to clean up. Sing a cleanup song (Resource Page 1). Then, ask them to see how quietly they can walk to the story area and sit down. You could have them put a finger to their lips and walk on tiptoe.

Gathering in God's Name

What you do: Begin with this opening. To teach about the Church Year, use the materials in the Church Year Worship Kit (see the introduction).

Say **Hi, boys and girls! Are you ready to sing a Jesus song?**

Sing "God Loves Me Dearly" (*LOSP*, p. 85; CD 9) or "All Hail the Power of Jesus' Name" (*LSB* 549; CD 1)

Invite the children to say the Invocation with you. Tell them "Amen" is the special word we say to ask Jesus to hear our prayers just like He promised.

Begin **In the name of the Father and of the Son and of the Holy Spirit. Amen.**

Offering Have a child bring the offering basket forward. Sing an offering song.

Pray **Dear Father in heaven, thank You for loving us and for making a wonderful place called heaven. Dear Jesus, thank You for dying on the cross to take away our sins so we are forgiven. Dear Holy Spirit, thank You for making us God's children so we can live with You in heaven someday. Amen.**

Celebrate Birthdays, Baptism birthdays, and special occasions

② God Speaks (20 minutes)

Story Clue

What you do: Allow the children to look at the people on Poster E.

Ask **Which of these people would you like to talk to or play with?** Accept answers. **Jesus died for all of these people and took away their sins. Which of them do you think will go to heaven when they die?** Accept answers.

Say **All these people can go to heaven if they believe that Jesus died for their sins, no matter how they look or where they live. Our Bible story today tells about heaven and some of the things that are in heaven.**

Bible Story Time

What you do: Display Poster F in such a way that the children can see it while you tell the story. To begin, cover the top half of the poster with a piece of paper, so only John and the angel show. Ask the children to help you tell the story today. Instruct them to give two claps each time you say the word *heaven*. Practice a few times before you start. An asterisk (*) indicates when to clap.

Note: Heaven is a difficult concept for young children to understand. Some of your children may also have had a grandparent or even a parent who has died. If they have questions, answer as simply and briefly as possible.

Say **One of Jesus' disciples was named John. One time, John was put on an island so he could not tell others about Jesus. But God loved John and all those who believed in Jesus. God wanted them to know that even though they had troubles, He was with them. He was making a home for them in heaven.*** Clap, clap. **So, God sent an angel to John in a vision. This vision was a special dream he had even though he was awake. The angel showed John what heaven*** (clap, clap) **would be like.** Point out John and the angel on the bottom of the poster.

In the vision, John saw Jesus with a bright light all around Him. Jesus told John to write a book that would tell everybody about heaven.* Clap, clap.

In the vision, John saw God sitting on a throne. Show Jesus on throne at top of poster, but keep the middle covered still. **John saw that everything bad had ended. There was a new heaven*** (clap, clap) **and a new earth. No one will get sick or die in heaven*** (clap, clap)**, and no one will cry or be sad!**

Then, John saw a beautiful city. Remove the paper covering the poster. **It had a huge high wall with twelve gates. An angel was at each gate. The city was made of gold, and the walls were decorated with all kinds of jewels. This city in heaven*** (clap, clap) **was the most beautiful place ever.**

The city in heaven* (clap, clap) **does not need the sun or moon or lamps to light it up because God is there. The gates will never be closed, and there will never be any night.**

Then, the angel showed John the river of the water of life. Point to it. **It was bright and shining, flowing from the throne of God right through the middle of the street. John also saw the tree of life.** Point to the tree on the poster. **This tree had twelve kinds of fruit—a new fruit each month.**

In heaven* (clap, clap)**, all the people will see God. They will worship Him. Everyone in heaven*** (clap, clap) **will be happy. People will sing and praise God and live in heaven*** (clap, clap) **forever and ever. The angel said to John, "Every person who believes that Jesus died to pay for sin will come to heaven*** (clap, clap) **after he or she dies."**

John wrote down all the things that he saw and heard. He wrote all of them in the Book of Revelation, the last book in the Bible. Because we sin, we cannot be good enough to go to heaven* (clap, clap) **all by ourselves. But God sent Jesus to die for all of our sins. When we believe in Jesus as our Savior, God forgives our sins and gives us the gift of eternal life with Him. We will live with John, the angels, other believers, and Jesus forever and ever. Isn't that wonderful?**

Key Point

Those who believe that salvation has been accomplished by the all-availing sacrifice of Jesus on the cross will bear the sign of Christ, written on their forehead in Holy Baptism, and they will have access to the tree of life.

Growing in Christ

Bible Story Review

What you do: You will need Lesson Leaflet 13 and crayons. Show Poster F, and review the story with the questions.

Ask **Who is talking to John?** An angel

What does the angel show John in a vision? Heaven

How will people feel in heaven? They will be happy because they are with Jesus; there will be no more sadness or hurts.

Who will be in heaven? Everyone who believes in Jesus as Savior

Hand out the leaflets and help the children draw lines from the pictures in the sidebar to the matching ones in the Bible story art. Talk about the shapes; have the children color the cross. On the back of the page, finish coloring the pictures and circle the ones that show something about heaven.

Option: After doing the activities on the leaflet, affirm that heaven is a happy place where all those who believe in Jesus will live with Him forever. Sing the following to the tune of "Are You Sleeping?"

Sing **Jesus died, Jesus died,**
For my sins, for my sins.
Now I can live in heaven, now I can live in heaven,
Forever, forever.

Bible Words

What you do: Read the Bible Words from 1 Timothy 2:4 in your Bible. Use the action rhyme to help the children learn the words.

Say **God says in the Bible that He wants everyone to hear the Good News about Jesus. God wants everyone to know that Jesus died for our sins. God wants all people everywhere to believe in Jesus so they can live in heaven someday. In heaven, all believers can sing and praise God. Let's say our Bible Words together.**

Use the following chant to teach the Bible Words. Repeat, inserting a different child's name or several children's names each time in place of "all people."

Say **[God]**   *Clap, clap.*
      [God] desires   *Clap, clap.*
      [God] desires [all people] to be saved.   *Clap, clap, clap.*

3 We Live (20 minutes)

Help children grow in their understanding of what the Bible story means for their lives. Choose the activities that work best with your class.

Growing through God's Word

What you do: Since young children need to move around and stretch their muscles, doing an activity that involves movement between sit-down times is especially helpful. When children use their large muscles, it also helps their brain process information. Use a beanbag or a beanbag animal to play a game with them.

Ask What do you think heaven will be like? Accept answers. **What do you think you will do when you are in heaven?** Accept answers.

Say We don't know exactly what heaven will be like because none of us has been there. But we know that heaven will be a beautiful, wonderful place. The Bible tells us some of the things that will be in heaven, like John saw in his vision.

In heaven, we will see God the Father, and we can talk to Him. We can talk to Jesus too. We will never be sick or sad in heaven, and we will live there forever. There will be many, many angels in heaven and all the people who believe that Jesus died for their sins. Heaven will be a happy place where we can sing and praise God. Won't that be great?

In the Third Article of the Apostles' Creed, we confess that we believe in the "life everlasting." Play this game with the children to help them remember things that they have learned about heaven: Have the children stand or sit in a line facing you. Explain that you are going to throw the beanbag to one of the children; that child will need to say something about heaven. Then, he or she will throw the beanbag back to you or to the next child. The next child says something about heaven. Have a few practice turns so the children understand what to do. Play long enough for all of the children to have a turn.

Craft Time

What you do: You will need Craft Page 13, stickers, and crayons. *Option:* Ahead of time, cut the page in half, fold both halves, and nest the pages together in order.

Say We are going to make a little book called *My Heaven Book*. This book tells about some of the things that we learned about heaven. If you did not do so ahead of time, show the children how to cut and assemble the booklets; help the children write their name on the front of the booklet. Read and talk about the pages, one at a time. Complete each page as described.

1. **In heaven, there are many angels.** Place the angel sticker on the page.

2. **In heaven, I will see Jesus.** Place the Jesus sticker on the page.

3. **In heaven, there is a tree of life.** Encourage the children to color the fruits different colors.

4. **In heaven, it is always bright.** Place the "God" sticker in the center of the page. Color the light rays yellow or orange.

5. **In heaven, everyone will be happy.** Place the happy-face sticker on the page.

6. **In heaven, people will praise God.** Color the musical notes.

7. **Someday, I will go to heaven because Jesus died and rose again to pay for my sins.** Place the cross sticker on the page. Have the children draw themselves by the cross.

Paper Plus option: Make a picture of heaven. Copy Activity Page 13B. Give the children crayons and markers to color the page and make the child outline look like them. Glue to construction paper to frame the picture, or help children cut around the picture and glue it to a paper plate. Punch a hole in the paper or plate to hang the picture.

Option: Give the children crayons to draw a picture on dark construction paper of what they think heaven will look like. Then have them paint the entire page with a mixture of lots of salt and water. When the water dries, their pictures will sparkle.

Snack Time

What you do: Make angel cookies, or use angel cookie cutters to cut out angel shapes from bread. Spread with flavored cream cheese. There are many angels around God's throne in heaven. Discuss how angels serve God and us.

Live It Out

What you do: Tell children to use their *My Heaven Book* to tell parents and friends about what they learned about heaven this week.

 **4 Closing** (5 minutes)

Going Home

What you do: Have leaflets and crafts ready to hand out. Cue CD.

Say **Today, we heard about heaven and what a beautiful, wonderful place it is. Someday, we will live in heaven with Jesus and all the angels. Jesus gives all those who believe in Him a home in heaven. Let's say that together.** Do so. **When we are in heaven, we will sing and praise Jesus for loving us and dying on the cross to pay for our sins.**

Sing "Chatter with the Angels" (*LOSP*, p. 20) or stanza 2 of "Jesus Loves Me" (*LOSP*, p. 42; CD 14)

Pray **Dear Jesus, thank You for loving us so much that You died on the cross for us. Thank You for making heaven a beautiful place where we can live with You, all the believers, and the angels forever and ever. Amen.**

Reflection

Did the children seem to understand that heaven is a wonderful place prepared by God for all believers? Were they confident that they would live in heaven with Jesus someday because He died for their sins?

Find and color the happy faces hidden in the picture.

Jesus Gives Me a Home in Heaven

Draw yourself next to Jesus.

Songs & Wiggles-Out Rhymes

Young children must use their large muscles and move around in order to process and learn new information. Incorporate music and movement between periods of quieter learning to allow for this. Give children scarves or ribbon twirlers to use as they sing.

Wiggles-Out Rhymes

Wiggles Out 1
Stretch up high.
Stretch down low.
Swing your arms to and fro.
Clap your hands, 1, 2, 3.
Then sit as quietly as can be.
Use actions to accompany the words.

Wiggles Out 2
Clap your hands for Jesus, 1, 2, 3.
He loves you, and He loves me.
Stomp your feet for Jesus; He's our King.
He can protect us from anything!
Wave your arms for Jesus, to and fro.
He is with us wherever we go!
Hooray! Clap and cheer.

Wiggles Out 3
Clap your hands and shout, "Hooray!"
We will learn of God today.
Stomp your feet and say, "Amen."
Jesus is our special friend.
Lean to the left; lean to the right.
Clap for God with all your might.

Getting Ready to Pray
Ten little fingers ready to play. *Wiggle fingers.*
Ten little fingers ready to pray. *Fold hands.*
Help me, dear Jesus, in every way *Bow head.*
To love and serve You every day. *Extend hands.*

Introducing the Bible Words
Here is the Bible God gave to me. *Open hands like book.*
What does He tell me? Let's look and see. *Shade eyes with hand.*
From Wiggle & Wonder, p. 28 © 2012 CPH.

Songs

Cleanup Song 1
Tune: "Row, Row, Row Your Boat"
Clean, clean, clean the room.
Put our things away.
Help, help, help, help—
Then we'll sing and pray.

Cleanup Song 2
Tune: "London Bridge"
Clean up, clean up, everyone,
Everywhere, everywhere.
Clean up, clean up, everyone,
Come, do your share.

Gathering Song
Tune: "Mary Had a Little Lamb"
Come and listen to God's Word,
To God's Word, to God's Word.
Come and listen to God's Word
From His book, the Bible.

Welcome Song
Tune: "Do, Lord!"
Welcome, we welcome, we welcome you today.
Welcome, we welcome, we welcome you today.
Welcome, we welcome, we welcome you today.
It's time to sing and pray.

Birthday Song
Tune: "London Bridge"
We're so glad that you were born,
You were born, you were born.
We're so glad that you were born.
Thank You, Jesus.

Baptism Song
Tune: "Mary Had a Little Lamb"
God chose [child's name] to be His child,
Be His child, Be His child.
God chose [child's name] to be His child
Through Baptism and His Word.

Snack Song
Tune: "London Bridge Is Falling Down"
Thank You, God, for food and drink,
Food and drink, food and drink.
Thank You, God, for food and drink.
How You love us!

Supply List

Every Week

Have a Bible, catechism, hymnal, children's songbook, Sprout or another puppet, and CD player for use every week, as well as classroom supplies such as scissors, glue, construction paper, stapler, hole punch, yarn or ribbon, and crayons or markers. Most lessons also include optional ideas that use a tablet device, smartphone, or laptop.

Other Supplies

Many of these supplies are for Welcome Time or optional lesson crafts. See each lesson to choose what you want to do; then, highlight the supplies you'll need to get.

Lesson 1
- ☐ Play dough, tree cookie cutters & toy figures
- ☐ Tissue paper & paper cups or construction paper
- ☐ Tree fruit

Optional
- ☐ Blocks
- ☐ Bathrobes & towels
- ☐ *Zacchaeus* Arch Book

Lesson 2
- ☐ Play dough & cookie cutters
- ☐ Green paper squares
- ☐ Craft sticks, spoons & bowls
- ☐ Plastic Easter eggs, items to shake & stickers
- ☐ Mystery bag, cross & paper crown
- ☐ Donkey (pool noodle, hobby horse, or the like)
- ☐ White T-shirt, blankets & palm branches
- ☐ Wide ribbon
- ☐ Stick pretzels & paper plates

Optional
- ☐ *Jesus Enters Jerusalem* Arch Book
- ☐ Toy figures & blocks

Lesson 3
- ☐ Items to count & sort
- ☐ Offering plate or basket & coins
- ☐ Small lunch bag with dollars & coins inside
- ☐ Pennies, stickers, or other gifts
- ☐ Gift bag or small box
- ☐ Vanilla wafers

Optional
- ☐ *The Widow's Offering* Arch Book
- ☐ Page protectors

Lesson 4
- ☐ Paper tablecloth or roll of paper
- ☐ Magazines
- ☐ Memory game items, tray & towel
- ☐ Communion chalice & plate
- ☐ Bows or ribbon
- ☐ Grapes & vanilla wafers

Optional
- ☐ *The Very First Lord's Supper* Arch Book

Lesson 5
- ☐ Play dough & cross cookie cutters
- ☐ Paper fasteners (brads)
- ☐ Heart-shaped cookies

Optional
- ☐ *The Night Peter Cried* Arch Book

Lesson 6
- ☐ Play dough
- ☐ Cross cookie cutters
- ☐ Construction paper circles
- ☐ Picture of Gethsemane
- ☐ Prepared piece of paper
- ☐ Paper fasteners (brads)
- ☐ Apple slices & fruit dip

Optional
- ☐ Props & story bag
- ☐ *The Week That Led to Easter* Arch Book

Lesson 7
- ☐ Tub of rice
- ☐ Plastic Easter eggs
- ☐ Paper plates
- ☐ Jelly beans
- ☐ Scarves

Optional
- ☐ Cups
- ☐ *The Easter Surprise* Arch Book

Lesson 8
- ☐ Plastic eggs & items to fill them
- ☐ Baskets
- ☐ Bread, jelly & cross cookie cutters

Optional
- ☐ Spices
- ☐ *John's Easter Story or Mary Magdalene's Easter Story* Arch Book
- ☐ Cross & crucifix
- ☐ Ribbon

Lesson 9
- ☐ Bibles
- ☐ Picture of Jesus

Lesson 10
- ☐ Play dough
- ☐ Cross & angel cookie cutters
- ☐ O-shaped pretzels or cereal

Optional
- ☐ *The Story of the Empty Tomb* Arch Book

Lesson 11
- ☐ Play dough & fish cookie cutters
- ☐ Buttons
- ☐ Easel, chalkboard, or desk
- ☐ Poster paper, paper cups & shoebox
- ☐ Netting or plastic bag & paper fish
- ☐ Heart & fish pictures
- ☐ Cross
- ☐ Fish crackers or bread, jam & fish cookie cutters

Optional
- ☐ Dish with cornmeal

Lesson 12
- ☐ Cookie sheets or plastic tablecloth & shaving cream
- ☐ Play dough & angel cookie cutters
- ☐ Dress-up items
- ☐ Cotton balls
- ☐ Travel items in a bag
- ☐ Toy car or picture of a car
- ☐ Marshmallows or pudding

Optional
- ☐ *Jesus Returns to Heaven* Arch Book

Lesson 13
- ☐ Small jewels & other decorations
- ☐ Pictures of beautiful or fun places
- ☐ Beanbag or beanbag animal
- ☐ Angel cookies or bread, cream cheese & angel cookie cutter

Supply List. Use with all lessons. *Growing in Christ*® Early Childhood © 2017 Concordia Publishing House. Reproduced by permission. This page is available on the Teacher CD.